U.S. Government houses of refuge were unique to the east coast of Florida. Ten were constructed between 1876 and 1886, but only Martin County's Gilbert's Bar House of Refuge survives.

GILBERT'S BAR HOUSE OF REFUGE

Home of History

SANDRA HENDERSON THURLOW
DEANNA WINTERCORN THURLOW

Published by Sewall's Point Company

for the benefit of the
Historical Society of Martin County
825 N.E. Ocean Boulevard
Stuart, Florida 34996
(772) 225-1961
and
Gilbert's Bar House of Refuge Museum
301 S.E. MacArthur Boulevard
Stuart, Florida 34996
(772) 225-1875

Printed by Southeastern Printing Company, Inc.
Stuart, Florida
Book designed by Deanna Wintercorn Thurlow
Cover photographed by Thomas H. Thurlow III
Copy proofed and edited by Noel Trachtenberg

ISBN 978-0-9630788-8-9

Library of Congress Control Number: 2007906126

The photographs in this book came from many sources. The late Susan Hall Johnson, whose father, Fred Hall, served at the House of Refuge during World War I, shared the very valuable photographs of U.S. Coast Guard exercises with the author many years ago. Her daughter, Jennifer Johnson Strauss, dug the originals out of storage so quality scans could be made. The late Elwin Coutant allowed me to make copies of photographs of his father and grandparents going about their daily activities at the Mosquito Lagoon House of Refuge. Numerous others shared their photographs. Their names appear after the captions. Many photographs were made from the negatives of local photographer Arthur Ruhnke that my husband and I purchased in 1989.

This book is a gift of the Thurlow family to the Historical Society of Martin County. My son, Todd Thurlow, took the cover photograph and provided his computer expertise. My daughter-in-law, Deanna Wintercorn Thurlow, designed the book, scanned the photographs and prepared the book for printing. She is the mother of three young children, so the gift of her precious time is monumental. The book could not have been done without her talent and generosity.

All of my passion for researching and sharing local history has the full encouragement and financial support of my husband, Tom Thurlow, Jr., who has been interested in local history since examining land titles and maps as a young lawyer in the early 1960s. He has spent endless hours critiquing my efforts and proofreading.

Sandra Henderson Thurlow
February 2008

GILBERT'S BAR HOUSE OF REFUGE
Home of History

OVERVIEW 1

ST. LUCIE ROCKS — HUTCHINSON ISLAND 7
    "THE CRUISE OF THE BLUE WING" BY JAMES A. HENSHALL 12

LIFE-SAVING SERVICE & SUMNER INCREASE KIMBALL 13

KEEPERS OF THE HOUSE OF REFUGE 15
    "FLORIDA SPORT" BY JOHN DANFORTH 22
    TRIBUTE TO HUBERT W. BESSEY 28
    SUSAN BESSEY'S MEMORIES 31
    "A TRIP TO GILBERT'S BAR STATION" 32

SHIPWRECKS 33
    J. H. LANE WRECK REPORT 34
    "HOUSE OF SHIPWRECKED MEN" BY HELEN VAN HOY SMITH 37
    "CAPT. REA'S WRECKS AT GILBERT'S BAR" 45

COAST GUARD YEARS 49
    "A STORY OF GILBERT'S BAR STATION NO. 207" 50
    JAMES HARRINGTON'S MEMORIES 55
    "THE NIGHT ADOLF HITLER HIT US FROM A SUB" BY ERNEST LYONS 58
    "OLDEST 'HOUSE OF REFUGE' HAS A HAPPY CREW" 63

AN ABANDONED BUILDING 66

THE CREATION OF A MUSEUM 68

A REFUGE FOR SEA TURTLES 71

THE EVER-CHANGING STRUCTURES 74

OBSERVATION TOWERS 81

LOUIS BARTLING 83

LIST OF HOUSE OF REFUGE KEEPERS 86

LIST OF COAST-GUARD-ERA MEN-IN-CHARGE 86

LIST OF MUSEUM-ERA KEEPERS 86

CHRONOLOGY 87

ENDNOTES 91

HOUSES OF REFUGE LOCATION MAP 95

GILBERT'S BAR HOUSE OF REFUGE — HOME OF HISTORY

(Florida Photographic Archives)

Overview

The history of the St. Lucie River region cannot be separated from the history of Gilbert's Bar House of Refuge on Hutchinson Island. The oldest building in Martin County, Florida, it was constructed before pioneers settled the area. In fact, the need for houses of refuge arose because the region was uninhabited.[1]

Ships taking advantage of the Gulf Stream that hugs the shoreline along the lower east coast of Florida were in danger of being blown off course during rough weather. Even if the dangerous off-shore reefs were avoided, shipwreck survivors who reached the beach found themselves in an inhospitable wilderness with no means of returning to civilization.[2] Consequently, in 1876, while the U.S. Life-Saving Service was still in its infancy, five houses of refuge were built on the lower east coast of Florida. Gilbert's Bar House of Refuge, built at the St. Lucie Rocks, was designated House of Refuge No. 2. The original five houses of refuge stretched along the coast from today's Vero Beach to Biscayne Bay. Ten years later, five more were built between today's Flagler Beach and the Indian River Inlet above Ft. Pierce.[3]

At houses of refuge, spaced at intervals along the unpopulated coastline, shipwreck survivors found shelter and sustenance. Keepers also helped shipwreck victims return to civilization. Houses of refuge, along with lighthouses, provided a governmental framework for the settlement of the East Coast of Florida.

Land for the first five houses of refuge was acquired with assistance from William H. Hunt of Biscayne Bay who became the local District Superintendent of the Life-Saving Service.[4] William Henry Hunt and William Henry Gleason were flamboyant lawyers who brought their families to the Miami River region in 1866, seemingly intent on using politics and their knowledge of land acquisition to set up some sort of empire in the wilderness.[5]

According to legend, the name Gilbert's Bar was given to a natural inlet south of today's St. Lucie Inlet in the mid-1800s because the pirate/slaver Don Pedro Gilbert periodically eased his ship, *Panda*, across the bar into the

Gilbert's Bar House of Refuge was built in 1876 when world commerce depended on sailing ships. During rough weather, boats were often blown off course and in danger of hitting the jagged reef that runs parallel to the shore. (Jennifer Johnson Strauss)

St. Lucie River to evade his pursuers and relax while preparing for his next venture.[6]

The location of House of Refuge No. 2 is described in official records as "at the St. Lucie Rocks, two miles north of Gilbert's Bar Inlet." Both names, "St. Lucie Rocks" and "Gilbert's Bar," began appearing on maps in the mid-1800s. The St. Lucie rocks are outcroppings of the Anastasia rock formation that underlies much of Florida.[7] The St. Lucie rocks protect Gilbert's Bar House of Refuge from erosion but aggravate the problems caused by salt spray. During a storm, waves dash on the rocks, explode skyward, and rain down on the roof of the House of Refuge.

Through the centuries, the narrow ridge between the Indian River and the ocean has attracted human beings. Archeologists have found evidence that the site of the House of Refuge was occupied by aborigines 4,000 years ago.[8]

Albert Blaisdell of Massachusetts, who received the contract for construction of the five original houses of refuge, completed Gilbert's Bar House of Refuge on March 10, 1876.[9]

Fred Whitehead, who took charge on December 1, 1876, was the first in a succession of Keepers who served at Gilbert's Bar House of Refuge.[10] Keepers who had families had the advantage of daily human contact. Families

OVERVIEW

also assisted in the search for victims of shipwrecks following storms. The lives of keepers and their families were lonely, but monotony was punctuated with terror, hardships and danger coinciding with shipwrecks.

In 1915, an era ended when the U.S. Life-Saving Service merged with the U.S. Revenue Cutter Service and the U.S. Coast Guard was created. At that time, Capt. Axel Johansen and his wife, Kate, were serving at Gilbert's Bar House of Refuge. Its name was changed to U.S. Coast Guard Station No. 207 and Johansen's title was changed from Keeper to Surfman No. 1.[11]

Coast Guardsmen, augmented by local young men in the Home Guard stationed at Gilbert's Bar during World War I, watched and patrolled the shore guarding against enemy invasion.[12] After the war, Coast Guard Station No. 207 no longer needed a full crew.

Buildings were constantly covered with salt spray and in need of paint and repair. Hurricanes wreaked havoc

At the end of World War II, Gilbert's Bar Coast Guard Station, the former House of Refuge, became surplus U.S. government property. Martin County commissioners officially began negotiations to purchase the building and 16.56 acres on June 11, 1952. (Thurlow/Ruhnke Collection)

through the years. Abandonment of Gilbert's Bar Station was considered following the locally-devastating hurricane of September 1933, but that was not to be. Instead, the house was moved 30 feet further away from the ocean and remodeled to allow for two large elevated cisterns.[13]

Station No. 207 regained importance as World War II loomed. Within months of the Japanese bombing of Pearl Harbor, German U-boats were torpedoing freighters off the Florida coast. Additional men were assigned to Hutchinson Island to patrol the beach, watch the skies, and guard against enemy invasion. In 1942, a new observation tower and mess hall were constructed.[14]

At the end of WWII, the former House of Refuge became surplus U.S. government property; it was decommissioned in 1945 and abandoned.[15] The Martin County Commission had officially opposed the decommissioning to no avail.[16] The old buildings became a picnicking destination for locals and a gathering place for artists and their students. People admired the building and its beautiful setting and appreciated its historical importance. The resolution requesting purchase of the House of Refuge was made by Commissioner Seymour Gideon and seconded by Charles Leighton on June 11, 1952.[17] Originally, the land was going to be used primarily for recreational purposes, but due to the vision of artist and museum specialist Charles Val Clear, the community began to realize the House of Refuge should be preserved because of its historical significance.[18] Martin County commissioners, with the help of Congressman Dwight Rogers and attorney Evans Crary, Sr., continued the lengthy process of acquiring the land from the federal government. The deed officially conveying 16.56 acres on Hutchinson Island and the former Coast Guard buildings is dated January 5, 1955.[19] The purchase price was ten dollars an acre, a total of $165.60.[20] Within months, the newly-formed women's organization, Soroptimist International of Stuart, facilitated the creation of the Martin County Historical Society in order to preserve and operate the House of Refuge as a museum. On May 10, 1955, the House of Refuge was leased to the Society for a museum and restoration began. The House of Refuge Museum was formally dedicated on December 9, 1956.[21]

OVERVIEW

In 2002, local artist Howard Schafer painted this historic view of Gilbert's Bar House of Refuge as it appeared in 1876 using historic photographs that showed portions of the structure before the porches were enclosed and the upper story was enlarged.

Ross Witham, a Stuart native who was among those working to establish a museum, found a baby loggerhead turtle entangled in seaweed and nearly drowned on the beach south of the House of Refuge. Although the hatchling did not survive, it inspired Ross to devote much of his life to sea turtle research. A program for hatching and releasing sea turtles developed simultaneously with the development of the House of Refuge Museum.[22] Work that began with the Florida Board of Conservation evolved into programs with the Florida Department of Natural Resources and continued until 1987.[23] Marine studies, particularly the sea turtle Head Start release program, overshadowed the historical mission of the House of Refuge Museum.

One rainy day when Steve Schmidt was the director of the House of Refuge Museum, he happened to run into Harmon Elliott, a winter resident from Massachusetts, in the Jensen Beach Hardware Store. He asked Steve, "What do you do when it's too rainy to fish around here?" Steve replied, "Mr. Elliott, come see our little museum." That chance meeting with Harmon Elliott eventually resulted in the building of the Elliott Museum, not only to honor and tell the story of Harmon Elliott's father, inventor Sterling Elliott, but also to house local history archives and exhibits.[24] Items exhibited at the House of Refuge were transferred to the Elliott Museum and the House of Refuge became a Maritime Museum.[25] Capt. Willard R. Laughon, a trustee of the Martin County Historical Society, facilitated the acquisition of 15 tons of surplus Navy material of historic interest.[26]

Museum director Janet Hutchinson was at the forefront of the effort that led to Gilbert's Bar House of Refuge Museum being declared an Historic Memorial in the State of Florida in 1969 and placed on the National Register of Historic Places in 1974. Subsequent restorations have been done with the view of preserving historic integrity.[27]

Major restoration of the buildings and the wall enclosing them took place after hurricanes Frances and Jeanne in 2004 forced the county to temporarily close the museum.

The wreckage of the lumber bark *Georges Valentine* was nominated to be a state underwater archaeological preserve in 2005, 101 years after it broke apart on the reef east of Gilbert's Bar House of Refuge.[28]

Gilbert's Bar House of Refuge Museum was a house of refuge within the U.S. Life-Saving Service for the first 40 years of its existence and then served as a Coast Guard Station for the next 30 years. After standing abandoned for ten years, it became the property of the citizens of Martin County in 1955 and has been a museum for more than 50 years. Gilbert's Bar House of Refuge, the last remaining of the ten constructed, has survived numerous hurricanes and several reincarnations to become a Martin County icon — a treasured "home of history."

ST. LUCIE ROCKS — HUTCHINSON ISLAND

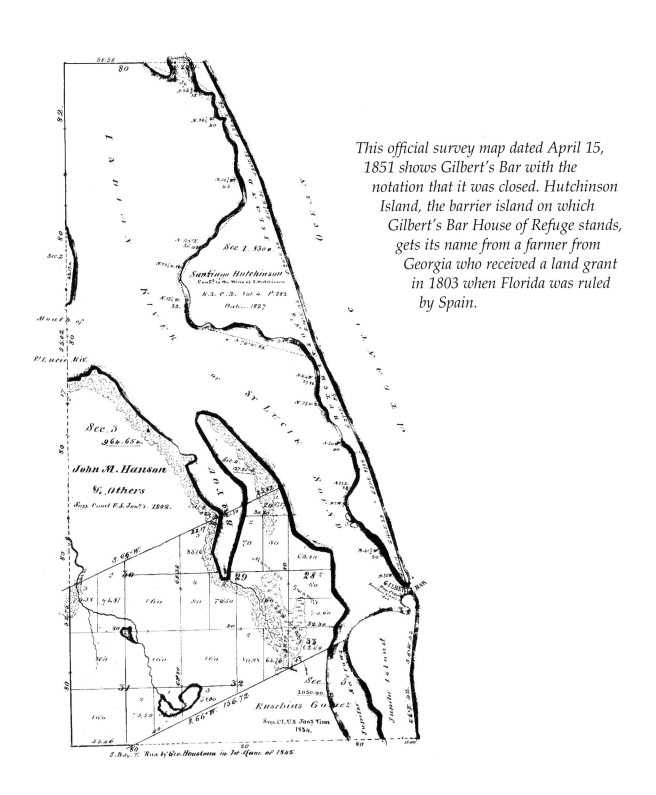

This official survey map dated April 15, 1851 shows Gilbert's Bar with the notation that it was closed. Hutchinson Island, the barrier island on which Gilbert's Bar House of Refuge stands, gets its name from a farmer from Georgia who received a land grant in 1803 when Florida was ruled by Spain.

side of Government Lot 2, Section 5 of Township 38 South, Range 42 East, the site of Gilbert's Bar House of Refuge, at the time occupied by the United States Life-Saving Service.³ The federal government granted Olds access easements across Government Lot 2, thereby allowing him to legally traverse the government land dividing his homestead parcels.⁴

Gilbert's Bar House of Refuge had become a Coast Guard Station by the time the mile-long wooden Jensen Bridge was opened in 1926.⁵ A road right-of-way between the beach access road at the east end of the Jensen Bridge and the Coast Guard Station was cleared in 1926 and improved in 1931.⁶ At some point in time, asphalt was put on part of the road, but by the time the House of Refuge Museum was launched only fragments of asphalt were left.⁷

In January 1956, when 2000 people attended the opening of the House of Refuge Museum, they traveled over the long Jensen Beach Bridge as dredges were forming the

This photograph was made when the right-of-way along the dunes from the Jensen Beach Bridge beach access road to Gilbert's Bar Coast Guard Station was improved in 1931. (Historical Society of Martin County)

ST. LUCIE ROCKS — HUTCHINSON ISLAND

Jensen Beach and Stuart causeways. The Old Beach Road, just west of the high tide mark on the sand dunes, still was the only way to reach the former Coast Guard Station.[8]

By January 3, 1958, when the "Bridges to the Sea" between Stuart and the Atlantic Ocean were dedicated, a new right-of-way for State Road A1A between the Stuart public beach and Jensen Beach had been secured and paved.[9] After James Rand's Tuscbay Properties, Inc. developed the southern tip of Hutchinson Island as Seminole Shores in the early 1960s, the old beach road was improved and named MacArthur Boulevard after General Douglas MacArthur, who Rand had hoped to hire.[10] In the 1970s, Indian River Plantation was developed and Seminole Shores was redeveloped as Sailfish Point. MacArthur Boulevard was reconfigured from its old route through today's Stuart Beach to pass through Indian River Plantation.

The "Bridges to the Sea" were completed in 1957. (Thurlow/Ruhnke Collection)

Camping and Cruising in Florida: An Account of Two Winters Passed in Cruising around the Coast of Florida, Robert Clarke & Co., Cincinnati, Ohio, 1888, pps. 75-76, by James A. Henshall, M.D.

Originally published as columns in Forest and Stream *and* American Field, *these paragraphs were written during the cruise of the Blue Wing in 1878:*

The 1878 Cruise of the Blue Wing

After spending a week in the delightful wilderness up the St. Lucie, we broke camp and proceeded down the river and across to the Life-Saving Station in charge of Jessee Malden. It stands on a high ridge, that is not more than seventy-five yards in width, and which separates Indian river from the sea. One can stand on the veranda of the station and cast a stone into the water on either side.

Along the beach is a barrier of dark coralline rocks, seamed and fissured, and worn into hollows and caves by the ever restless sea. Beyond is an out-lying reef, where the rollers break and form long lines of foam-crested combers, which chase each other in rapid succession and come tumbling and dashing on the rock-bound shore, thundering and roaring through the rents in the caverns with, truly, an awful sound, causing the very earth to tremble beneath one's feet. By moonlight the scene is singularly beautiful, wild, and impressive.

The U.S. Life-Saving Service & Sumner Increase Kimball

Sumner Increase Kimball was born in Lebanon, Maine, in 1834 and graduated from Bowdoin College in 1855. He was admitted to the bar in 1858, the same year he was married. He soon moved to Washington and began his career with the federal government as a clerk in the Treasury Department. His energy and ability attracted the attention of the Secretary of the Treasury, and in 1871 he was appointed to head the Revenue Marine Bureau that was within the Treasury Department.[1]

Investigations revealed that life-saving stations, which were within the Revenue Marine Bureau's authority, were ineffective and in poor condition. In spite of this, they were able to save numerous lives and a great deal of property. Seeing the need, Congress appropriated an additional $200,000 to be expended for life-saving purposes through the Revenue Marine Bureau.

Immediately, Sumner Kimball began the challenging work which would occupy him for the rest of his life. He was a bureaucratic genius and applied an orderly system. Kimball worked tirelessly and his successes justified his request for more funds and expanded authority. After a thorough investigation, recommendations were made to construct 23 new life-saving stations, 22 lifeboat stations, and five houses of refuge.

Sumner Increase Kimball was Superintendent of the U.S. Life-Saving Service from its inception in 1878 until it was merged with the U.S. Marine Bureau in 1915 to become the U.S. Coast Guard. (U.S. Coast Guard)

The report stated: "Upon the coast of Florida the shores are so bold that stranded vessels are usually thrown high enough upon the beach to permit easy escape from them; therefore the usual apparatus belonging to the complete stations are not considered necessary. The section of that coast is almost destitute of inhabitants, and persons cast up upon its inhospitable shores are liable to perish from starvation and thirst, from inability to reach the remote settlements."[2]

The report recommended that five houses of refuge should be built. These houses of refuge, all built in 1876, were each large enough to shelter 25 persons and stocked with sufficient provisions to support them for 10 days.

Because of Sumner Kimball's outstanding leadership, the U.S. Life-Saving Service became an autonomous organization separate from the Revenue Marine Bureau in 1878. In 1886, five more houses of refuge and a life-saving station at Jupiter Inlet were constructed. Sumner Kimball remained at the helm of the U.S. Life-Saving Service for 37 years until it was merged with the Revenue Marine Bureau to form the U.S. Coast Guard in 1915.[3]

Keepers of Gilbert's Bar House of Refuge

The Life-Saving Service seldom encountered difficulties in finding applicants for the job of keeper.[1] Southeast Florida was a wilderness in 1876 when five keepers were needed for the newly built houses of refuge. Men applied for the job because it offered a well-built home and an annual salary of $400.[2] Money was hard to come by in pioneer southeast Florida. Ten years later, when five more houses of refuge were constructed, the keeper's job was still coveted.

Keepers had several basic duties: to reside constantly at their stations; to take custody of and care for the station's property, for which they could be held accountable; and to govern the station and its premises. They served as ex-officio inspectors of customs and guarded government interests over dutiable goods carried on wrecks until other customs officials arrived. The law made them the guardians of wrecked property until relieved by its owners or by receipt of instructions from their superiors.[3]

House-of-refuge keepers and their families traveled the shore in both directions after storms in search of shipwreck victims. The regulations of the Life-Saving Service required a daily log to be kept, of which weekly transcripts would be sent through the district superintendent to the General Superintendent. In addition, immediately after any wreck occurred, the keeper furnished a complete report of every detail of the disaster to his superiors. Making a false statement in the log or reports made the keeper subject to dismissal.[4]

Fred Whitehead, who was the first Gilbert's Bar House of Refuge Keeper, was an Englishman mentioned by Charles W. Pierce in *Pioneer Days of Southeast Florida*. We know that he had a wife and a son Freddy. He served as an assistant lighthouse keeper at Jupiter Lighthouse for a few months before he was appointed Keeper of Gilbert's Bar House of Refuge.[5] We also know that he was a photographer because he wrote a letter published in *Anthony's Photographic Bulletin* in July 1877. In it he complained, "I pursue photography here under difficulties. I live right on the beach and salt spray is everywhere."[6]

The second Keeper, Ezra Stoner, was a single man who, according to the U.S. Census of 1880, was born in Ohio and was 65 years old. It also said that he was paralyzed.[7] The same census report mentions that Preston McMillan was also living at Gilbert's Bar House of Refuge with his wife, Clara, and one-year-old son Albert. Official correspondence reveals health issues required McMillan to assist Ezra Stoner and ultimately relieve him of his duties. According to the census, Preston was 26 years old and was born in North Carolina. Clara Huston McMillan was 18 and was born in Florida, as were her parents.

Preston McMillan was the son-in-law of John Carroll Houston who was the Keeper of House of Refuge No. 1 located at today's Vero Beach. Keepers drawn from such a small population were often connected by blood, marriage, friendship or business.

Jessee Maulden, a plume hunter who came to the Lake Worth area with his wife in 1872, filed official reports as acting Keeper of Gilbert's Bar House of Refuge during the times Fred Whitehead, Ezra Stoner and Preston McMillan were listed as the official keepers. He was also on duty during a visit from Dr. James Henshall when his party passed through in 1879. Henshall, a renowned sportsman, published an account of his visit in *Camping and Cruising in Florida*.[8] Maulden, like Fred Whitehead, had served as an assistant lighthouse keeper at the Jupiter Lighthouse. Consequently, he had experience working for the government and was in the network of local settlers who were employed by the U.S. Life-Saving Service as house-of-refuge keepers. Living at the

All houses of refuge had decorative porch rail braces like those in this 1906 photograph of Bethel Creek House of Refuge. (Wilson Price)

Gilbert's Bar House of Refuge probably gave him the opportunity to decimate local rookeries.[9]

The Brown family, also mentioned in Charles Pierce's *Pioneer Life in Southeast Florida*, relieved the McMillans. Mrs. Brown, whose family had settled on Lake Worth, walked the beach to House of Refuge No. 3 to assist the Pierce family after the birth of Charles's sister, Lillie.[10] Mr. and Mrs. Brown and several of their children lived at Gilbert's Bar House of Refuge before they gave up Florida pioneering and moved to Washington State.[11]

John Thomas Peacock, who is listed as the Keeper of Gilbert's Bar House of Refuge for the early part of 1885, came from the Ft. Lauderdale House of Refuge where he also served for a short time before securing the Keeper's job at Biscayne Bay House of Refuge No. 5, which was in his own neighborhood. "Jolly Jack" Peacock, as he was called, served at Biscayne Bay House of Refuge with his wife and large family for a number of years. Before working for the U.S. Life-Saving Service, Jolly Jack served as the Sheriff of Dade County as well as Collector of Revenue and Assessor of Taxes for Dade County. Keep in mind that the 1880 census of Dade County, stretching from the Keys to the St. Lucie River, listed only 194 people and the 1885 census listed only 332.

According to the 1885 Census of Florida, Samuel F. Bunker, who followed Jolly Jack Peacock as Keeper of Gilbert's Bar House of Refuge, was a 29-year-old farmer who was born in New York of parents also born in New York. One can deduce a bit about him by reading his detailed report of the wreck of the *J. H. Lane*.

David McClardy, Gilbert's Bar House of Refuge Keeper from June 1888 to July 1890, cannot be found in a U.S. Census, perhaps because the 1890 U.S. Census of Florida was lost in a fire. No information about David McClardy has surfaced. In contrast, a great deal of information is available about the next Keeper, Hubert W. Bessey, who is credited with being Stuart's first settler. Transcriptions of articles published long ago give the reader insight into the nature of the man who is one of the St. Lucie River region's most esteemed pioneers.

Alan W. Shaw, the son of H. B. "Harry" Shaw, Life-Saving Service District Superintendent, is responsible for

---

Keep in mind that the 1880 census of Dade County, stretching from the Keys to the St. Lucie River, listed only 194 people and the 1885 census listed only 332.

These photographs of the Coutant family at the Mosquito Lagoon House of Refuge are the only known views of everyday life inside a House of Refuge. At left, Capt. Samuel Coutant is sifting flour and, above, Louisa Coutant works beside a cast iron stove. Opposite page: The young man by the phonograph is Harold Coutant who moved to Stuart and married Edna Witham, Ross Witham's aunt. (Elwin Coutant)

supplying information about Axel Johansen, who became Keeper of Gilbert's Bar House of Refuge following Hubert W. Bessey's resignation in December 1901. In 1910, Alan Shaw enlisted in a government construction force similar to the Seabees of World War II. He was assigned to Gilbert's Bar House of Refuge where he served many happy months working under the direction of Captain and Mrs. Axel Johansen who he grew to love and respect. Many hours were whiled away with storytelling. The Shaw family lived in Ormond near today's Daytona Beach. Alan Shaw included the following in an article found in the Halifax Historical Society files: "A Norwegian ship's Captain lost his ship with all hands during a severe hurricane off the Florida East Coast in the 1880s. He floated for five days on a wooden hatch cover that just barely kept him afloat, and all the last day, drifted within sight of shore, but he was too weak to attempt to swim, so tantalizingly drifted all day just too far out to try and make it to shore. But that next night, the hatch washed ashore - but the poor man found that he was unable to walk, so he crawled up above where the tide would reach and covered himself with beach sand to keep warm. In the morning, he started to crawl northward, and was discovered by two daughters of the house-of-refuge Keeper of the Chester Shoal Station, who summoned their father, and the poor man was taken to the Station, where eventually he was nursed back to health. This man was Captain Axel Johansen, who had 'gone to sea' at the age of ten, as a cabin boy and had spent all the rest of his life on shipboard. When he was sufficiently recovered, he returned to Norway, and intended to continue in his lifelong profession of sailing the old square-riggers, but two things happened. First, the Age of Steam was coming of age and few more of the older 'tall ships' were being built. And being an old-school man of the sailing age, he had no wish to change and try to master steam navigation. Then again, he couldn't forget his experience on the Florida Coast, so he sold all his holdings in Norway, took passage to America,

traveled to Florida, and made his way to Chester Shoals House of Refuge. After a short time there as a guest of the Keeper and his family, he married the Keeper's oldest daughter. And fortunately just then there came an opening for a new house-of-refuge keeper, and Captain Johansen and his new wife, Kate, received the appointment and spent the rest of their lives in that capacity, looking after ships and boats in trouble."[12]

It appears from U.S. Life-Saving documents that men who wanted the position of house-of-refuge keeper placed their names on lists with the U.S. Life-Saving Service district superintendent. When an opening arose, the district superintendent recommended the most qualified man for the job. Sometimes, in order to get their "toe in the door," men would have to take a position more distant from their homes than desired and would be moved to the more desired location at a later date. This seems to be the case with William Rea of Stuart who served at Biscayne Bay House of Refuge before being transferred to Gilbert's Bar House of Refuge in January 1903. With the back-to-back wrecks of the *Georges Valentine* and the *Cosme Colzaldo* the following year, Captain Rea had more

Susan Bessey stands on the dock at Gilbert's Bar House of Refuge with her sister Bessie Shackleford sitting beside her. Their father, W. A. Corbin, sits on the porch. This photograph, taken by Mr. and Mrs. Will Harris of Walton, in 1898, is the best known photograph of Gilbert's Bar House of Refuge before the upper row of windows were added around 1911. (Historical Society of Martin County)

KEEPERS OF GILBERT'S BAR HOUSE OF REFUGE

shipwreck activity than any other house-of-refuge keeper in the history of the U.S. Life-Saving Service.

William Rea and his wife, Harriet, like Hubert and Susan Bessey, were local pioneers. Consequently, more is known about them than the other keepers. William Rea, the son of a physician, was born in Hackettstown, New Jersey, in 1851. William received his education at nearby Morristown College, then went into the retail drug business. In 1894, he and his wife purchased land on the St. Lucie River and tried their luck at pineapple cultivation.[13]

John H. Fromberger, who followed Capt. Rea, had once been First Mate and cook on the schooner *Corinne* used for district superintendent H. B. Shaw's quarterly inspections. Before coming to the Gilbert's Bar House of Refuge, he served at the Fort Lauderdale House of Refuge, where his wife, Agnes, gave birth to their son, Henry.[14]

The last Keeper at Gilbert's Bar House of Refuge was Axel Johansen. He and his wife, Kate, the daughter of Orlando Quarterman, the only Keeper of Chester Shoal House of Refuge, were on duty when House of Refuge No. 2 became U.S. Coast Guard Station No. 207 in 1915. Kate and Axel remained at Gilbert's Bar for three more years.[15] With a crew of young Coast Guardsmen on site, their lives and duties changed and loneliness was a thing of the past.

with a crew of young Coast Guardsmen on site, their lives and duties changed and loneliness was a thing of the past.

Lollie Roebuck and Reginald Kitching sit on the steps of Gilbert's Bar House of Refuge in 1914 where they spent their honeymoon as guests of Axel and Kate Johansen. Another Stuart couple, Josephine Kitching and John E. Taylor, who were married on March 10, 1914, also spent their honeymoon at Gilbert's Bar House of Refuge. (Carol Mann Ausborn)

GILBERT'S BAR HOUSE OF REFUGE — HOME OF HISTORY

More than a century ago, John Danforth, a hunting and fishing guide who alternated between Maine and Florida, wrote wonderful articles in Shooting and Fishing, *published weekly in New York City. This article mentions Gilbert's Bar House of Refuge, Hubert Bessey, the boats built by the Bessey brothers, sea turtles, pioneers on the St. Lucie River and the region's abundant wildlife. Including John Danforth's story in this book brings to light the long-buried article found in the Boston Public Library by Robert W. Cook, author of* Chasing Danforth, A Wilderness Calling.

"Florida Sport" by John Danforth
Shooting and Fishing Christmas Number
December 15, 1898

There is no greater pleasure for a backwoodsman than to have the privilege of writing accounts of his hunting, fishing and exploring trips for the Christmas number of *Shooting and Fishing*. It is a pleasure to sit and speculate on which of the many interesting trips he has taken will be the one to choose. So it is this time, and after going over more than a dozen all fresh to the mind as they were at the time they happened, I have decided on one which happened in 1898 in Dade County, Florida. My wife and myself, in company with Ben Crafts, were living on board a twenty-five-foot cabin sloop, which had all the conveniences of a shore camp. We cruised on the Indian River, but most of the time we spent on the St. Lucie River and its tributaries.

Our sloop was built by the Bessey brothers especially for cruising in the Florida waters. The Bessey brothers are educated gentlemen, who have modeled and built nearly all the sailing craft owned by Gilbert's Bar Yacht Club, and in our sloop they seemed to get as near perfection as one could ask. We had plenty of room for cooking, eating, sleeping and to carry fresh water, provisions, and tackle of all kinds. We had an outfit, so we could leave the sloop anchored, with the cabin locked, and go for a cruise in the woods for days. My object in securing such a boat was not for catching and killing all we could find, but to better support myself and

John Danforth's sloop, Caribou, *built by Hubert and Wilbur Bessey, "had plenty of room for cooking, eating, sleeping and to carry fresh water, provisions, and tackle of all kinds."* (Robert W. Cook)

family by becoming a guide for gentlemen who visit Florida for sport.

At the time of which I write the *Caribou* (our sloop) lay at anchor about a half mile off the mouth of Huppee creek in the full moon of June. I had planned to be on the ocean beach at night to welcome the big turtles which come there to deposit their eggs in the sand where they hatch. When their work is done they disappear and are not seen again until the next year at about the same time. From where we lay at anchor to the U.S. Government house of refuge was eight miles across the Indian River. At the house of refuge it was only a stone's throw from the Indian River to the

Atlantic Ocean. The wide sand beach extended north and south as far as the eye could reach and was a good place for turtles to come.

We hoisted the mainsail, then the anchor, and as the *Caribou* moved out Ben set the jib. With the stiff breeze that was blowing we were soon bowling along at lively speed, and it was only a short time when I called Ben to let go the jib. We hove to just off the house of refuge, took in the mainsail, let go the anchor, and soon had things snug for the night. Ben shelled oysters, my wife lighted the gasoline stove, and in a short time we had an oyster stew that was what Ben called "real filling."

While we were eating H. W. Bessey came aboard and did not hesitate to take a bowl of stew and also a plate of broiled pompano, with a cup of chocolate and cream. Mr. Bessey told us the turtles were on the beach the night before in small numbers, which encouraged us. After supper Mr. Bessey left us to go to the post office, four miles away. He expected a letter from his wife, who was in Tennessee for the summer. Just as the sun was sinking among the pine trees and looked like a silver ball in a bucket of blood, we walked to the beach and went to one of the many lots of sea shells which are thrown up by the ocean storms and piled into huge drifts. There we sat down and admired the beautiful colors and shapes of the many varieties of shells, waiting for night to come and the turtle to show up.

A backwoodsman can fully enjoy a sunset scene on the shell-covered beach of Florida's east coast. He will see all the colors in the sky, all the tinted curling waves, and breathe the soft cool air; but to tell it as he sees it is beyond his power. He is all absorbed in the gifts of his Creator, and wonders how cities are built and thousands of human beings swelter in heated apartments, when the world is so large and there is room in the cool pure air for all. While his mind is working on such hard questions time passes and out of the ocean comes the moon. In a few minutes the scene is all changed. A dull gray covers all, and then a silvery brightness which grows stronger; dark shadows appear, and the night is on.

We get up and look south along the water's edge; then to the north, but could see no moving objects. The noise of the

> *A backwoodsman can fully enjoy a sunset scene on the shell-covered beach of Florida's east coast...but to tell it as he sees it is beyond his power.*

waves breaking on the shore sounded louder than before night. We walked along the beach, going north. Traveling was good and it was a pleasure to stroll by moonlight. We had walked about a half mile when we saw a black object near the water far ahead. We hastened forward and soon found our first turtle. When we got to within twenty yards of the turtle we stopped and watched its movements. Mr. Bessey had given us information in regards to their actions. He said, "Don't disturb them until they lay their eggs; then when they start for the water run forward and turn them. Don't get into their mouths; if you do they will cut you badly."

The turtle went back from the water about seventy feet, and with its big flippers dug a hole in the sand about eighteen inches deep, into which it laid its eggs. While it was at that work it seemed to notice nothing. A black bear came along the beach looking for fish. It paid no attention when it saw or scented us as it ran over the ridge and disappeared in the mangrove swamp which lay all along the Indian River. We watched the turtle very closely, and when it started for the water we made a grand rush for it, Mrs. Danforth crying at the top of her voice, "Look out for that mouth."

When Ben and I reached the turtle it was within thirty feet of the water. We made a bold dash for the flippers, Ben taking the forward, and I the hind one on the same side. As we grabbed I said, "Now together, let us turn him." We lifted with our whole strength, expecting to see the turtle turned on its back; but it was not so. We never got the flippers a foot from the sand when the mighty strength of the turtle threw us about, rolled Ben over in the sand, who was soon on his feet and into the struggle again. In the meantime we were all nearing the water, and just when we thought we had our prize at our mercy, a huge roller came in and thundered down upon us. The cooling effect of the water broke our hold and the turtle disappeared from sight. Mrs. Danforth stood at the water line when the big wave came, and as we were panting, came up the beach she said, "Are you hurt? Ain't those turtles big fellows? I am glad he got away. Don't try another. Let us go back to the *Caribou*. You cannot use one if you turn it."

But we did not do all she asked, for after we had talked and rested a while, we went to where the turtle had put her eggs, dug away the sand that was over them, and took out 183 eggs. They had soft shells, white in color, round as marbles, and about one and three-fourths inches in diameter. We continued our walk along the beach, and within a half mile came upon another turtle which we had but little trouble in turning, as it was a small one, measuring only three feet across the shell. For a while we watched the struggles of the turtle as it tried in vain to turn itself back; then we started back to the *Caribou*, taking our eggs along with us.

Early the next morning Ben and I were again on the beach, and went to our helpless turtle. On the way we saw where several turtles had been out, and we could have got hundreds of eggs, but we let them all rest where they were. The turtle we dressed and took with us to the sloop.

On our way back we met Mr. Bessey and told him of the tussle we had with the big turtle. He laughed and said that was the big fellow which so many had tried to turn, and that we were very lucky that we did not get hurt.

For our breakfast we had an omelette made from twenty of our turtle eggs, and it was fine. We all liked it, and Ben went back on to the beach and dug out another nest, which we put into the locker. We then called goodbye to Mr. Bessey, and with all sails set, we soon rounded Sewall's Point and lay our course for a long run up the broad St. Lucie River. Mr. Britt, the man who attends the draw in the railroad bridge at Stuart, knows the *Caribou*, and we did not have to blow the conch. The wind was fair and we passed through the draw at good speed. Mr. Britt looked down from the key and said: "Danforth that is the best all-round boat I ever saw." A half hour later we rounded Bessey Point, and taking the wind on the other quarter, we went flying up the south prong of the St. Lucie. We sailed along just outside of the little docks which extend into the river from packing houses where the planters put up their pineapples for the northern market. We passed Corbett's, Dyer's and Taylor's dock and at each place we were saluted and they would say, "Come in and get some apples." At Taylor's dock we landed and got about a barrel of his choice apples. He asked if we had seen the school of manatee which was in the bay. We had not. He said he

John Danforth

thought there were twenty. We left Taylor's dock and headed for the Halpattiokee River, two miles south. Before we reached it we ran into the school of manatee, which were feeding in about five feet of water. What a commotion they made! Ben and Mrs. Danforth were on the forward deck with harpoons looking for sawfish, and when the Caribou plowed into the drove they sent a deluge of water over both of them, and soon both were in the cabin with their eyes perfectly round. I think there was a quarter of an acre of that river which was like some huge pot filled with water and boiling over. At the rate we were going we were soon beyond them and entered the wood-bordered river.

Up from the mouth about two miles we dropped anchor, and for several days we watched the alligators. We could have killed many. Nearly everyday we came upon a group of Seminole Indians, who would always say, "You buy venison me? You buy turkey me? You buy hog me?" If you took any of what they had to sell and asked the price, it would always be "Ten cent you," meaning it was ten cents a pound and they never had any chance to weigh a thing. Their way was to cut off a portion and say. "Five pounds you," when it might be four or eight pounds. We soon learned to get good weight when we bought of them.

We lay at anchor only a few days when we ran down and out of the South Prong bay, where we could lay at anchor away from the shore, so we could sleep. The creatures in the woods and water kept up such a rumpus we could not sleep up the river where we lay. A few days later found us again at our camps, where we welcomed our friends and told them about our trip.

Illustration by George Potter from Camping and Cruising in Florida *by James A. Henshall*

INDIAN RIVER.

The following tribute to Hubert W. Bessey, a charter member of Gilbert's Bar Yacht Club, located several hundred yards to the south of Gilbert's Bar House of Refuge, was read at the club's annual meeting held January 11, 1919.

A Tribute to Hubert Bessey

Hubert Wilbur Bessey was born on a farm near Milton, Wayne County, Ohio, on December 17, 1855. He was the son of Abnah and Margaret Ellenberger Bessey, and was the last of a family of six children. His brother, Dr. Charles E. Bessey, Professor of Botany at the University of Nebraska, died in 1915, and his only surviving sister, in 1916.

The Bessey family was of French extraction, the original form of the name being Besse. The tradition is that the early members of the family, who were Huguenot, were compelled on account of religious persecutions to flee to England from the old home near Strasbourg in Alsace. This exodus occurred in the latter part of the 17th century, after which the "y" was added to the name.

A few years after the death of the father, in 1863, the family moved to Oberlin, Ohio, and it was there, at Oberlin College, that Hubert Bessey received the greater part of his education.

After completing his college course, he taught school for a time, but his love of nature, and outdoor life influenced him to join a surveying expedition going into southern Texas and Mexico, and for two years he was engaged in this work.

In 1881 he came to Florida, stopping at Ormond. There he bought a sailboat, and started down the Indian river, looking for a suitable place to locate.

The location and water advantages of Stuart decided him in its favor. He was the first settler, taking up a homestead in what is now Bessey's addition to the town of Stuart. For several years he engaged in raising pineapples, devoting his spare time to boat building.

Transportation being so difficult and uncertain in those early days, he gave up the pineapple business and

*Hubert Wilbur Bessey
(Historical Society
of Martin County)*

took charge of Gilbert's Bar House of Refuge. Here he continued his boat building, and many boats along the Indian River were evidence of his skill in that line.

On February 19, 1885, he married Miss Susie Corbin, of Nashville, Tenn.

A few years later the railroad, having come through Stuart, he again undertook the cultivation of pineapples and in January, 1901, returned to Stuart to live, occupying the Danforth Hotel.

For three years he and his wife had charge of this place, and it was through his influence that Grover Cleveland, Joseph Jefferson, Daniel Lamont, Dr. Joseph Bryant, and later George W. Perkins, came to Stuart.

In 1904, he built one of the most attractive homes on the St. Lucie River and lived there for several years, selling it in 1910 to George W. Perkins.

In 1910, Mr. Bessey, through Mr. Perkins' influence, became identified with the Palisades Interstate Park, and for eight months of the year devoted his time to this work.

In the summer of 1917, he undertook, in connection with his park work, the management of a large fish industry at Rockport and Gloucester, Massachusetts. On account of his health, it was his intention when he left Stuart, in April 1918, to give up the park work, and spend the summer in Rockport, where his duties would not be so arduous.

But the war conditions having made such inroads in the park organization, he was asked to continue as its superintendent, giving all extra time to the Rockport business. Though in poor health, his sense of duty and loyalty would not permit him to refuse, and for four and a half months he gave himself to this double work. He died very suddenly at the Guest House, Palisades Park, New York, on September 17, 1918.

He was buried at Nashville, Tenn., the home of his wife who survives him. No child was born of this marriage.

Mr. Bessey was one of the charter members of Gilbert's Bar Yacht Club and was always much attached to it and took great interest in its welfare and proceedings and contributed much to its success.

Therefore be it resolved by said Club, assembled at this, its regular annual meeting:

1. That it highly appreciated its late, lamented member, Hubert W. Bessey. His was a personality singularly modest, engaging and charming. A man of great breadth of sympathy and interest, a mind unusually well stored with general and accurate information, and being altogether dependable and reliable, a man of the highest integrity, the circle of his friends was limited only by those whose privilege it was to know him. We can truly say of him, that his demise was a great loss to this club, for, 'He was a man, take him all in all, we shall not look upon his like again.'

2. That we extend our heartfelt sympathy to his bereaved family.

3. That these resolutions, with their preamble, be spread upon the minutes of the Club, as a perpetual tribute to and memorial of Hubert W. Bessey.

4. That the Secretary be and is hereby authorized and directed to have these resolutions and their preamble published in the West Palm Beach, Fort Pierce, and Stuart newspapers.

Gilbert's Bar Yacht Club on Hutchinson Island (Errol Willes)

The following interview with Susan Bessey was published in the Stuart News, *July 23, 1954. She died the following November.*

Susan Bessey's Memories

"In 1893 a call for teachers for Florida was made through the teachers' bureau at Nashville. A friend of mine accepted a position at Rockledge and she urged me to join her, but my father would not consent to my coming to this 'wilderness.'

"I finally accepted a position to teach at Fort Tibbals with nine pupils enrolled. En route I stopped in Rockledge a few days; then I took the train to Eau Gallie, the terminus of the Florida East Coast Railroad, where I took the boat of Captain Bravo, having been given a letter directed to him. We landed at the Merwin dock on Sunday morning and was met by Mr. Walters, the school supervisor. He suggested I go to church where I met many people of the community. During my stay in Eden I boarded with Mr. and Mrs. Will Richards. He was considered the Pineapple King in this section. It was the custom in those days to have dances at the packing houses and it was there I met Hubert W. Bessey.

"After school closed I went home to Nashville, Tenn. I did not return to Eden that fall, and Mr. Bessey and I were married Feb. 19, 1895 at the home of my father, W. A. Corbin, in Nashville.

"After a few days visit with Mr. and Mrs. Richards in Eden, we went to the House of Refuge where we spent seven happy years."

Susan Corbin Bessey in 1922 (Taylor/Ashley family)

This account of an outing to Gilbert's Bar House of Refuge not only mentions Capt. Bessey but two of his boats, Goose *and* Robinson Crusoe. *The* Goose *was constructed for Homer Hine Stuart for whom Stuart is named and the* Robinson Crusoe *was built for Budd and Len Gardner who lived just south of Portuguese Joe on Hutchinson Island for whom today's Joe's Point is named.*

A Trip to Gilbert's Bar Station

A jolly crowd of merry-makers left Tyler's dock Saturday at 2:30 for a trip to Gilbert's Bar Station, on the cat boat, "Goose," with a box of provisions, and a keg of water for refreshments, and a music box, the music keeping time to the merry chatter aboard. Our party consisted of eleven, leaving out the cat, viz.: Mr. and Mrs. Olmstead, Miss Piety Hair, Mrs. Dora Tubbs and her little daughter, Vera, and her cat Tip, Mr. Frank Everett, Mr. Len Carlton, Mr. D. Carlton, Mr. Reuben Carlton and Master Perry. On their arrival at Eden they found a nice warm supper, prepared by Mrs. Len Gardner, on the yacht "Robinson Crusoe." After partaking heartily, they proceeded on their way, arriving at the station at 11:30 p.m. The genial keeper, Mr. Bessey, aroused, and dancing commenced, followed by a moonlight stroll on the beach, and retiring at 3 a.m. In the morning they were awakened by the most delightful music proceeding from the aforesaid music box, and played by a master hand. After breakfast, a dip in old ocean, another stroll on the beach, exploring those rocks and caves, which were a sight worth seeing, our party returned well satisfied with their trip and making plans for another in the near future. One of the greatest features of the trip was the beautiful songs rendered by Mr. J. F. Olmstead.

NELLIE BLY
East Coast Advocate, October 3, 1890

An early Indian River sailboat photo taken by Lloyd C. Hill (Thurlow Collection)

shipwrecks

When shipwrecks occurred, the lives of house-of-refuge keepers and their families, which were normally lonely and monotonous, suddenly became perilous and exciting. Although the keeper's job was to give succor to shipwreck victims once they were stranded on land, keepers occasionally had no choice but to do their best to make rescues at sea. Such was the case with the wreck of the *J. H. Lane*. Keeper Samuel Bunker's Wreck Report makes exciting reading. Having the accounts of both Keeper William Rea and his wife, Harriet, gives a unique glimpse of life at Gilbert's Bar House of Refuge during a very unusual time. Never in the history of houses of refuge did back-to-back shipwrecks occur except at Gilbert's Bar House of Refuge in October 1904.

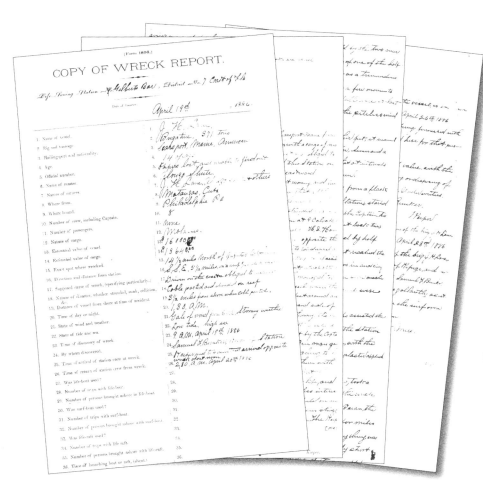

A copy of the wreck report for the J. H. Lane

GILBERT'S BAR HOUSE OF REFUGE — HOME OF HISTORY

Keeper Samuel F. Bunker's Report of the Wreck of the J. H. Lane, *April 27, 1886*

The brig *J. H. Lane* traveling from Matanzas to Philadelphia, with a cargo of molasses, was driven on the coast and obliged to anchor 2 ½ miles S.S.E. of this Station on the evening of the 16th of April 1886 during a severe storm from the eastward. The Keeper of the Station discovered her at seven o'clock the next morning and immediately went down the beach until arriving opposite the brig, he saw that although pitching heavily, she was all right as long as the cable held, having good holding ground. At 1:30 a.m. April 19, the brig's cable parted and she stranded on a reef three quarters of a mile from shore. The Keeper discovered her condition at 9 o'clock the next morning, during a slight cessation of the rain, and accompanied by H. A. Hawley and Chas Wolf started immediately for the scene of the disaster arriving opposite the wreck about 11 o'clock, they found that the vessel

The brigatine J. H. Lane *(Historical Society of Martin County)*

had listed well over to wind ward and lay quartering to the waves that washed clear over her decks. At 1 p.m. the Keeper and assistants saw that the men on board the vessel were attempting to launch a small boat, which after about an hour's hard work they succeeded in doing successfully, and all managed to get into the boat without accident, but they had no sooner cast off from the vessel when the current, which set very strong to the southward, whirled the stern of the boat around and drifted her past the stern of the vessel, a huge wave from the starboard side of the vessel caught the boat broadside on and she immediately capsized throwing the men in every direction. They all succeeded in regaining the boat that was bottom side up and were enabled to hold on to her by means of the life lines, that by the Captain's oversight had been fastened securely around her at bow and stern, one man gave out soon after leaving the vessel and was drowned, the others clung to her with desperate energy. A breaker would now and then sweep over them with such resistless force that they would be torn from the boat, but they would bravely swim back to her again, It was indeed a battle for life, and the Keeper and his assistants watched them with almost breathless interest expecting every moment to see the struggle ended, but they held on until, after having floated two miles south of the wreck and had been struggling in the water for nearly two hours, they at last neared the shore. The Keeper having one end of a line fastened to him, the other end held by the two men above mentioned, rushed into the surf, and catching hold of one of the half-drowned men, shouted to his assistants to haul ashore, just as a tremendous wave broke over them there was a desperate struggle for a few moments but they were pulled ashore in safety. In this manner all were at last saved, and taken over the bank to shelter them from the pitiless wind that still blew with great violence.

Cold, wet, some hardly able to stand on their feet, it seemed hardly possible that they would be able to reach the Station, seven-and-a-half miles distant, and the nearest shelter from the rain that at intervals would pour down upon the already chilled and half dead men.

The Keeper, after giving each of them each a drink of brandy from a flask that he had fortunately put into his pocket when leaving the Station, started the men upon their long and tedious journey. After assisting the Captain to within one-and-a-half miles of the Station, The Keeper went back two miles after his son, who had sunk exhausted to the beach, and by half-carrying half leading and stopping to rest every few steps at last reached the Station arriving there at 2 a.m. and having been nine hours in making a distance of seven-and-a-half miles, a good fire and hot coffee soon made the shipwrecked men feel better, and the Keeper and his assistants were glad enough when they at last could get a little sleep.

Too much praise cannot be given the two men who assisted the Keeper in rescuing, and helping the crew of the ill fated brig to the Station.

The Shipwrecked men all felt pretty well the next morning, with the exception of one man who had difficulty in breathing. A mustard plaster applied to his chest by the Keeper soon relieved him.

About three o'clock the Keeper, Captain and some of his crew, took a sailboat and sailed down the river until they had arrived opposite the wreck when, crossing over the land that lay between the river and Ocean, the first sight that their eyes rested upon was the beach, covered for miles with debris. The brig had broken up during the night and everything was piled, twisted and mixed up together in inextricable confusion, only short pieces of the standing rigging could have been saved and they would have been but for being five miles down the beach.

The Captain and his crew left the Station April 26, 1886, having been sheltered six days at the Station, and being furnished with provisions from the government stores, that are placed here for that purpose.

The Captain failed to save anything of much value, with the exception of the boat or yawl, and failed also in selling or disposing of the wreck, which I am holding as far as possible for the underwriters.

SHIPWRECKS

There was a general call for safety pins when the rescued crews of two vessels, which came to shore within 24 hours, were garbed in outfits stored away 20 years before in the House of Refuge, at Gilbert's Bar, near Stuart, Fla.
By Helen Van Hoy Smith, July 24, 1932

House of Shipwrecked Men

A house crowded with shipwrecked men greeted Mrs. William E. Rea when she returned to her home near Stuart, Fla. following a visit to Atlanta in 1904. In the fall of that year storms of hurricane intensity swept the east coast of Florida, and various ships went to the bottom. Among these was the *Georges Valentine*, which sank after fighting the storm for three days.

At Gilbert's Bar, near Stuart, the government maintained a "House of Refuge" as a shelter for storm victims, and Mrs. Rea's late husband was keeper of this "House."

"I was in Atlanta myself at the time of the shipwreck," said Mrs. Rea, recalling incidents connected with the storm, "but I came home the day after receiving a wire telling me what had happened. And I found the house full of the shipwrecked men, for the day after the Valentine went down another vessel was wrecked and fifteen additional men made their way ashore."

In Mrs. Rea's home at Stuart is a book issued in 1905 by the government and containing reports made during the previous year by houses of refuge and life-saving stations. It gives a thrilling account of the wreck of the *Georges Valentine*, which was an Italian vessel weighing 822 tons. When hit by the northwest gale, which "struck with the force of a West Indian hurricane" the vessel was en route for Buenos Aires with a cargo of lumber.

"Under scant canvas," the report continues, "plunging and tossing, the heavy seas pounding her bow and breaking over the weather bulwarks, she kept on working her way warily to the northward through the coral-fringed Straits of Florida, with their threatening indraughts and numerous counter currents which tend to baffle the ever cautious mariner. As time wore on, conditions continued more threatening when on the third day (October 16), the tempest raged with increased violence, a terrible squall of wind accompanied by torrents of rain, knocking the vessel down helplessly while each successive sea made clean breech over her as she was swept away to leeward, lost amidst dense clouds of fine feathery spray.

"The master, fully realizing the perils of the shore vainly endeavored to get his vessel by the wind, but her sails would not bend and the heavy sea throwing her bow in the trough of the sea, she continued to drift before it until after nightfall when the storm gave evidence of subsiding, the storm sails were hauled out with the hope of getting her heading offshore, but being unable to take care of herself, continued to drift steadily to leeward at about 8 p.m. The roar of the surf and the screaming of breakers close aboard and discernible gave the first signs that danger was imminent. In another moment her stern pounded heavily on the bottom in the shoal water, her bow swung aft, and getting before the wind, the doomed craft was driven straight for the shore, rolling her decks in under the breakers that engulfed her. She struck with

The wreckage of the Georges Valentine *that broke apart near the House of Refuge on October 16, 1904 attracted settlers and tourists for many months. (Florida Photographic Archives)*

terrible force, her three steel masts falling almost simultaneously, while the din of grinding and crunching metal, parting of wire rigging and gear and slatting of sails rent the wind, thundered above the storm.

"On board the unfortunate *Valentine* was a crew of twelve men. When her masts went by the board, they sought refuge as best they could, but found no shelter for her hull was broken open, and the sea rushing through her groping sides with tremendous force, lifted the deck house, boats and decks clear out of the ship flinging the terrified crew into the breakers and the mass of wreckage and floating timber piling up along the edge of the surf. One man was instantly killed, having been stuck on the head by a falling spar. The others struck out, buffeted by the sea and knocked about by the wreck stuff, hoping to reach a place of safety. Seven of the crew were cast up on the beach, bewildered, bruised and bleeding, while the less fortunate, struggled in vain to gain the shore, the outlines of which were dimly visible. These were never afterward seen. Victor Erickson, a very powerful swimmer, was first to reach the shore. Scantily clad, chilled and well-neigh exhausted he groped his way along the beach in quest of succor.

"While these tragic incidents were taking place, the *Valentine* was totally invisible from the shore. At Gilbert's Bar Station, a house of refuge, isolated on a narrow strip of desolate coast, a solitary keeper, maintained his vigilant watch to seaward apprehensive for the safety of the seafarer abroad that night.

"'That solitary keeper, of course, was my husband,' said Mrs. Rea, taking up the thread of the story." The Swede, Victor Erickson, came bringing with him a shipmate he had found and rescued. My husband gave them brandy and put them to bed. The rest of the night he spent walking the beach. By dawn five more men had been rescued while clinging to floating timber.

"Their clothes were in tatters and they were so chilled and exhausted that they were unable to speak. One of the men was so badly cut on the face and throat that his tongue could be seen through the cruel slashes.

Capt. William Rea with visitors on the wreckage of the Georges Valentine *(Florida Photographic Archives)*

"That next day while my husband was still giving aid to these men the Spanish ship *Cosme Colzado* was stranded three miles north of the Station. One man became entangled in the rigging and was drowned, another swam to the beach with a small line and then hauled a three-inch rope ashore by which all the rest landed in safety.

"That night when I arrived from Atlanta I found twenty-two shipwrecked men in our small house, and you can readily see that there was plenty to do. We had no radios, telephones or electric lights and we had to go nine miles to Stuart for food and for doctors. After the men from the Valentine recovered somewhat, the problem of giving them all clothes was one that caused us some worry and amusement, too. In fact looking back over the affair there was much that was ridiculous but at the time it was happening it wasn't funny.

"Up in the attic were five outfits of clothing which had been sent 25 years previous by the Women's Relief Association. Each consisted of a suit of underwear, the old fashioned two-piece long-legged and long-armed variety, one shirt, one pair of trousers and a coat. These five outfits had to clothe 22 men. Obviously if a man had underwear, he couldn't have trousers and a shirt, but we managed to clothe each one more or less adequately, if not artistically. Then the fabric of the clothes, having been sent 20 years previously, began to give away and there was a general SOS call for safety pins.

"The crew of the *Valentine* all chose gauze underwear as they had been almost literally skinned alive. They had been in the sea with the cargo of lumber and their poor bodies were rubbed raw. They suffered intensely, but it was really remarkable how rapidly they recovered.

"By choice they slept out in the boat house. We wanted to give them beds, but they complained that mattresses and springs were too soft. They preferred to roll up in blankets and sleep on the floor.

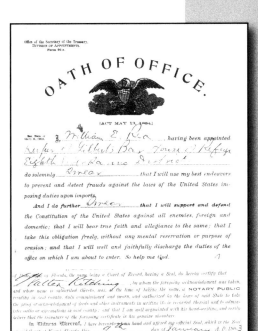

"The master of the *Valentine*, Captain Mortola, was a well educated man, and was always most gallant. He called me 'Lady Rea.' The second mate was also a man of education, but the rest of the men were rough and ready fellows. The crew of the *Valentine* remained with us about 3 weeks but the 15 men from the Spanish ship stayed only a short time as the consul immediately provided them with transportation.

"The government allowed us 25 cents a meal, two meals a day, for each foreign shipwrecked man we took care of. This service was for the benefit of aliens only, not a penny was provided for Americans, as this country had relief agencies for its own people. We were supposed to give men good plain food but were not required to provide either sugar or butter. Naturally we did not have the heart to carry out these regulations and the men from the *Valentine* soon developed excellent appetites.

"I had a dishpan that held fourteen quarts. Every day this was filled with spaghetti, canned tomatoes and canned corn beef and seasoned highly. The pan just fit on the top of a small woodstove. The men were not lazy and were certainly interested in food. They gathered up drift wood for fires and did the cooking and dishwashing. There was a Russian who was a born housekeeper. When he actually lifted up the wood box and swept behind it, my heart warmed to him.

A couple stands on the St. Lucie Rocks at the site of the wreck of the Georges Valentine (Florida Photographic Archives)

"Fishing also provided amusement for our shipwrecked men and they would dress the fish and throw them in the pan with the rest of the mixture.

"When their cuts and bruises began to heal, I really think they enjoyed life, but of an evening we could hear them talking among themselves mournfully and solemnly. We naturally thought that they were grieving for their mates that had been drowned and the good ship that had gone down but my husband found out differently. He learned enough of their jargon to discover that instead of mourning for their companion they were bewailing the loss of a pig that they had been fattening for a feast in Rio. They never seemed fully to get over the loss of this pig, and the further loss of ship's biscuits. The mate had made them eat old ones before opening the new case and the case was to have been opened the day the storm came up.

"After a while the various consular agents were contacted and transportation was provided for the men, who represented five different nationalities. When they left I found I didn't have a rug fit to put down on the floor, the men had slept in all I had. Then too I missed some solid silver knives and spoons that were valued as heirlooms in my husband's family, the forks were all there and I couldn't imagine what had happened to the knives and spoons but we found every one of them.

They were out in the boat house, stuck up in odd places. The knives had been used to open the cans in a case of clam chowder that had been there. Every can had been eaten. I suppose the chowder helped assuage the grief of the ship wrecked men over the loss of the pig and hard tack.

"I received postal cards from Captain Mortola from many different ports. On one of them he wrote, 'I now take marriage.' The Russian stayed around here in Stuart for a good many years and fished for a living.

"Those two shipwrecks are the only ones that ever occurred near Gilbert's Bar. The House of Refuge was established about 1830. It was just about to be abandoned when these storms occurred.

"When I lived there the ocean was my front yard and the river my back yard. But I did have some flowers growing about in tubs and buckets. I had a lovely rose bush that bore beautiful blossoms. I had rooted it from a bouquet that had belonged to Mrs. Grover Cleveland. The waters near Stuart teemed with fish and Ex-President Cleveland used to spend some time here in the winter. Mrs. Cleveland came with him in 1903 and it was then that I got the rose cutting. She was very gracious and friendly. She always attended church every Sunday, and it was a matter of comment that she seemed to dress in finer clothes than we of the village could afford."

Mr. Rea owned valuable pineapple plantations and after serving for five years at Gilbert's Bar, became one of the best known growers in the section. Mrs. Rea continues to live in Stuart where she takes great pleasure in raising tropical shrubs and flowers.

Capt. Rea's Wrecks at Gilbert's Bar
Stuart Messenger, September 5, 1918

Capt. W. E. Rea was formerly in charge of Gilbert's Bar Life-Saving Station, popularly known then as the House of Refuge — this was away back in the year 1904, before the present nine husky, uniformed Coast Guards strolled the Atlantic beach between the St. Lucie inlet on the south and "as far as possible on the north" — that was Capt. W. E. Rea's beat, and he didn't always wear his uniform, although he had one, and the regulations were very stiff.

In Capt. Rea's many seaside experiences with an all powerful and stormy ocean, the night of October 16 will live longest and most vividly in his memory. A gale from the northeast had been blowing and getting harder every hour each day. The captain had seven shipwrecked sailors on hand to feed and there he was marooned on the strip east of Sewall's Point, for his boat had broken its moorings.

The vessel struck at night, 300 feet east of the House of Refuge. The captain was in bed. There was a tap on the window and a voice on the porch, and in broken Swedish and rasping Scottish two voices said, "We're shipwrecked, let us in." The captain got up, slipped on his clothes over his nighty, opened the door, when in came a giant Swede, the first mate, and a little Scotchman, the blacksmith, with two ribs broken and his neck twisted. They didn't have much on and Capt. Rea gave them clothing. Then the planks began smashing up against the House of Refuge and the waves and the rain divided honors in trying to get inside. Capt. Rea lit his lantern, gave it to the Swede, told him to stay ashore, perched up as high as he could on the lumber, and if anything happened to the captain, who was going out over the lumber, to try and find some of the rest of the crew, then the mate was to come on out and help the captain ashore. Here was a gale and a blinding rain, chilly almost to the point of freezing, a

Life-Saving Service Seal (National Archives)

ship on the rocks and its lumber, nearly all 3 x 9 planks, was coming ashore flat, sideways, endways and in flying broken pieces. But Capt. Rea kept dodging and climbing as the sticks whizzed by, looking for men who might be washed ashore. He found the captain, one-fifth of the skin off his body, whose first remark was "My master, the rocks are bad." Only one of those fellows is left in this neighborhood, big Ed Smith, a fisherman down at the inlet, who has changed his name from the original Yiddish cognomen, Sarkenglov. As the survivors were picked up no regrets were made about the shipmates, but they mourned the "new ship and new bread," for they had been fed on old biscuits and now the stock was exhausted and if the new ship had not been wrecked the next day they would have been put on rations

The Scotchman with the broken ribs was in a bad way. Everybody called the blacksmith "Shorty." He was getting worse, there was an abdominal swelling that required attention. Capt. Rea brought him over to Stuart. The train to the St. Augustine Hospital had gotten here first and the conductor was about to pull the bell cord when Capt. Rea hailed him, pointed to the suffering sailor on the cot, and explained his predicament as captain of the House of Refuge with the dying man on his hands and no money to pay this fare. "Nothing doing," said the conductor. "Can't ride without a ticket." Beville was agent then in the two little old shanties now down at Salerno. Capt. Rea shouted to Beville to bring him a ticket. Beville dived into the freight house after it, Rea started on the run to get it. The conductor pulled the cord, the train started. Rea ran out with the tickets, the train was gone, so was the Scotch blacksmith. Capt. Rea was wild, but the situation cleared when somebody said Capt. Bessey paid his fare. Superintendent Parrot said later the conductor was right, but everybody in Stuart said he was wrong.

Capt. Rea gave an order and later Mr. Bessey's money was returned. The entire crew including everything in their "ditty" bags, had two half-pennies and the old Scotchman had a watch which was still running when his bag floated ashore.

For a long time at the House of Refuge the captain and his good wife, who was housekeeper and mother to all the wrecked sailors for those stormy days had been for a long time at their wits end in packing and unpacking and airing twenty complete outfits for men and women, which had been supplied in all manner of clothing by the Woman's Sailor Relief Society of New York. But now how thankful they were for this varied wardrobe, for the twelve men in the crew of the *Georges Valentine,* an Italian barkentine, were without clothing. Seven were saved and five were lost. And there was a big, fat pig on board, which they were feeding up for Christmas at Rio de Janerio, where they were bound. The buzzards and and the coons found the pig in the sand later. The ship had cleared at Pensacola, had sailed down until they saw the lights in Havana, when the gale struck them and they turned around in the Gulf stream headed north, and never afterward were able to come about. Capt. Prospero Martalo some time later surprised Mrs. Rea by sending a postal card from Italy. The information it contained was simply this, "Dear Mother, I have news to tell you; I take marriage."

About the cargo, H. S. Witham and Will J. Dyer bought the lumber and they sold dock stuff all through the county for years.

But the next day after the *Georges Valentine* went ashore was the 17th of October, and three miles north of the House of Refuge is the prettiest piece of sand on the East Coast and that same lovely beach had been selected by the *Cosme Colzado,* a Spanish ship in ballast from Gloucester, Mass. to Brunswick, Ga. She could not get in Brunswick on account of the heavy fog in the bay which they didn't have a knife on board sharp enough to cut and the northeast gale pounded them down the coast against the Gulfstream, and when they tried to sail out they made leeway faster than headway, and in 24 hours after striking, the vessel was pounded to pieces. Of the crew of sixteen, one was drowned and nine were injured and at 2 p.m., when they struck, the rain was so hard and thick they could not see a hundred feet in any direction. When the crew made shore, they simply went ahead with the wind at their back until they struck the Indian River a few rods away and by good luck they were directly in line with a negro hut owned by "Harvey" who operated a truck patch. He kept the Spanish crew till they ate him out of house and home. Then Capt. Rea took them and kept them for a week. "And that week," said Mrs. Rea, as she broke in on the captain's story, and her face beamed on the reporter, "that week was full of fun." One of the Spaniards proved to be a splendid cook, but the assortment of pigeon English if put in shape would have been Esperanto. I couldn't get them to come to dinner, they didn't understand the English word, and I didn't know theirs. Finally, in desperation I took one comical fellow by the sleeve and led him to the dining room and pointed to the steaming dinner and said "dinner." He opened his eyes and raised his arms and shouted "bunjge" and what a rush they all made for the table."

The Spanish consular agent at Pensacola proved to be impossible. His superior was worse if that is possible, and I finally had to tell him "to go to the devil," said Capt. Rea, "and I found relief for this crew as for the *Georges Valentine* through the British consular agent at Jacksonville. In these two crews we had Scotch, Russian, Italian, Spanish and Swedish, and they were all as naive a lot of men as ever came ashore. When I finally got them off to Jacksonville the men stood up and the captain put his arms around me and said, " 'Master, good-bye, we no more see you.' "

Coast Guard Years

The U.S. Coast Guard era started in 1915 with the merger of the U.S. Life-Saving Service with the U.S. Revenue Cutter Service. Gilbert's Bar House of Refuge became Coast Guard Station No. 207. Since the nation was at peace, the duties of Axel Johansen, who continued to live at Gilbert's Bar with his wife, Kate, did not change appreciably, but by 1917, the United States had entered World War I. A crew of five men joined Axel Johansen at Gilbert's Bar Station and, before the war was over, local boys, as members of the Home Guard, augmented the men who had come from different parts of the country.

After WWI, surveillance relaxed and various Coast Guardsmen served at Gilbert's Bar Station with their families much as the House-of-Refuge Keepers had served before them. Things changed as international tensions intensified and the U.S. entered WWII with the bombing of Pearl Harbor.

A mess hall and new observation tower were built at Gilbert's Bar Coast Guard Station in 1942. There was a constant rotation of new recruits who patrolled the beach and watched the sea and air, reporting whatever they saw to higher authorities.

Lawson Zeigler, whose mother and stepfather owned Bentel's Bakery in Stuart, poses in his U.S. Coast Guard uniform around 1918. (Garnett Early)

Josephine Taylor visits Capt. and Mrs. Johansen at the House of Refuge after it became a Coast Guard Station. (Taylor/Ashley family)

GILBERT'S BAR HOUSE OF REFUGE — HOME OF HISTORY

The Stuart Messenger, Stuart, Palm Beach County, Florida, Friday, July 20, 1917 (Consolidated with Stuart Times March 2, 1917) An interesting story entertainingly told of this isolated home, out in the ocean away from mainland.

A Story of Gilbert's Bar Station No. 207
U.S. Government maintains Coast Guard Crew there two miles out in the ocean

Since our northern friends of the hotels and cottages of last winter left us for colder and, as we learned from the weather reports, a more unforgettable climate, we have made great changes in Stuart and its conveniences, and the United States government has thought us deserving of a trained crew of Coast Guards. They are now on duty at Station No. 207, known as Gilbert's Bar, off the mouth of the St. Lucie river or just outside the junction of the Atlantic ocean, the St. Lucie river and the Indian river, near where boats enter the Jupiter Narrows. The station stands on a narrow strip of land, separated from the mainland by the Indian river and east of another strip known as

Capt. Axel Johansen, at left, stands with his crew at Coast Guard Station 207 in 1917 or 1918. From left, Axel Johansen, W. I. Baker, Lawson Zeigler, Earl J. Ricou, Shelby McCulley, L. J. Walker, Harold Wybrecht, Fred Hall and Veril Silva. (Verdimay McCulley Stiller)

COAST GUARD YEARS

Earl J. Ricou, wearing his Coast Guard uniform, poses in front of Gilbert's Bar Yacht Club that stood on the beach south of Station 207. (Chee Chee Ricou Gunsolus)

Sewall's Point. The low coastal ridge on which the house stands is a short stone's throw in width and the abrupt rocky ocean front is elevated 17 feet above the sea level. In front of the station is Gilbert's Bar lying out in the ocean about two miles or more northeast to southwest, and in the shallowest places showing only two feet of water. It is eight miles long and lies directly across the mouth of the St. Lucie, a splendid harbor in a navigable stream, soon to be the outlet at St. Lucie Inlet of the canal from Okeechobee. The House was built 40 years ago and "The House of Refuge" was the only shelter anywhere on the wild low-lying coast for the wrecked mariner. Seventeen years ago Capt. Axel H. Johansen succeeding Capt. Bessey, was the keeper, and his relief watch was Mrs. Johansen, a true Floridian, born near Titusville and trained from girlhood in a House of Refuge where her father was keeper. Mr. Johansen, from Norway, landed in Seattle, came to Florida and is now again in charge of 207, with a sturdy crew of five powerful young men who go by numbers when on duty. Their names as recorded in the Government Service are.

No. 2: C. F. Maldt, Chatham, Mass.
No. 3: F. M. Loy, Council Groves, Kans.
No. 4. W. L. Baker, Seville, Florida
No. 5: E. W. Evans, Chatham, Mass.
No. 6: J. C. Paterson, Georgia

Their isolated home is owned, fitted and furnished by the United States government, and reports are made weekly to the Treasury Department at Washington through the superintendent of the Eighth District Coast Guard at Jacksonville. These surfmen draw good wages, $65 per month, and 30 cents per day grocery allowance, or a wage of $74 per month. They club in together and buy what they like best to eat and "Mother" Johansen is the chef. The supply boat is buoy in a business way, and the self-bailing life boat is ready to be shoved off when needed.

In order to show our friends of the fresh water interior and the back woods farther north what is to be done by these salt water experts who are at work all the time, we give the work program:

DAILY ROUTINE BILL
6 a.m.: Rising bell
6:30 a.m.: Breakfast; uniform for the day announced at breakfast
7-8 a.m.: Cleaning hour
8 a.m.: Inspection
8 a.m.-Noon: Drill hours
Noon: Dinner
1 to 4 p.m.: General work about the station
7 p.m.: Privilege hour for retirement to those not on duty
8 p.m.: Inspection; See all lights out except station lights (if needed)

DRILLS
Monday: Fire drill; International Morse code and semaphore signals
Motor boat laws; beach; apparatus drill (first month)
Tuesday: Boat drill; International code signals; and pilot rules and regulations (for preventing collisions)
Wednesday: International Morse code; semaphore signals; and Coast Guard regulations, etc.
Thursday: Beach apparatus drill; International code signals and compass, etc.
Friday: Boat drill; resuscitation; International Morse code and semaphore signals drills
Saturday: General cleaning; general muster, second Saturday each month (See Articles No. 1818, Regulations for the Coast Guard.) Air all bedding

CLEANING BILL
Surfman No. 2: Surfboat; station
Surfman No. 5: Cleaning dining room and kitchen
Surfman No. 6: Assists No. 4 in filling and cleaning lamps, lanterns, etc.

FIRE DRILL
Surfman No. 1: Having general supervision
Surfman No. 2: Provides fire extinguisher

A sign with "207," the number designated to Gilbert's Bar Coast Guard Station, was placed on the dune for the benefit of airplanes. This photograph was probably taken in 1918 when Earl J. Ricou served in the Coast Guard on Hutchinson Island. (Chee Chee Ricou Gunsolus)

COAST GUARD YEARS

Coast Guard Seal

Coast Guard Shield

Surfman No. 3: Provides buckets of water (in absence of regular equipment)
Surfman No. 4: Same work
Surfman No. 5: Same work
Surfman No. 6: Same work

The idea of the Coast Guard Naval service at Station 207, Palm Beach County (St. Lucie County line is 30 feet north of station), is to answer signals of distress, furnish assistance and relief, be on the lookout for wrecks and vessels out of the course and warn them off dangerous places. The Guards were recently put in the service and especially instructed to watch the coast for alien enemies and suspicious landing parties or strangers who do not belong there. Watches are changed every four hours, day and night. The clock is punched every half hour and a complete and scientific record is kept of the temperature, barometer, and conditions of the weather regarding rain, wind, squalls, and changes indicated.

The last wreck report Keeper Johansen sent from this life-saving station was the loss of the Barkentine St. Paul bound for Matanzas, foundered four miles out north of the station last November. The crew of eight was saved, cargo of $56,000 and value of vessel $30,000 total loss. He took the men to Stuart, telegraphed the owners, gave the crew dry clothing and left them in charge of their captain.

April 20th, 1917, Captain Johansen enlisted five men for extra duty as lookouts in the service of Uncle Sam. They have their duty to do in emergencies, are equipped to go to the limit and (report censored). Are they lonesome? No. They have no time to play ball or get lonesome. The formulas of work to do and how and when to do it in signaling, boat drills, motor boats and pilot rules, resuscitation, storm warnings and "dangers that may arise" keep them wide awake and with one eye open when asleep.

The first light to the north is Canaveral, 90 miles north, and to the south Jupiter, 16 miles away and to the south. Fort Lauderdale is the next station.

If you have any papers or magazines to send, address them to Surfman No. 1., in charge Coast Guard Station No. 207, Sewall's Point, Fla.

GILBERT'S BAR HOUSE OF REFUGE — HOME OF HISTORY

The photographs of Coast Guard training on Hutchinson Island were shared by Susan Hall Johnson, the only child of Fred Hall, who served at Coast Guard Station 207 in 1917 and 1918.

54

COAST GUARD YEARS

A visit to Gilbert's Bar House of Refuge Museum in 1995 prompted James W. Harrington, of Hazelton, Pennsylvania, to write the following account of his Coast Guard duty during World War II.

After enlisting in the United States Coast Guard on September 5, 1942, I was assigned to Curtis Bay Training Station in Maryland for four weeks of basic training.

At the conclusion of basic training in early October of 1942, I was assigned to duty at Gilbert's Bar House of Refuge in Jensen Beach, Florida. Arriving at the House of Refuge (via Fort Pierce) along with me were a number of enlistees from my Curtis Bay basic training group, including among others:

William R. West, Scranton, PA
Leslie Dale Keyser, Bloomsburg, PA
Joseph P. Stetina, Summit Hill, PA
Stephen Vanno, Summit Hill, PA
Norman Jefferies, Lansford/Summit Hill, PA

For the next six months, those of us quartered at the House of Refuge lived out of our sea bags and slept on canvas cots. I don't recall any formal furnishings except for a recreation room.

Our duties, under the direction of a Chief Petty officer, were to report any planes which passed over our area. Records were kept of the number of planes, how many engines a plane had, its altitude, and its direction. This data was then relayed by phone to an information center in Miami.

Duty hours were subdivided into four on and eight off. The four duty hours consisted of two hours in the observation tower and two

After their hours on watch, Coast Guardsmen enjoyed the pleasures of fishing, swimming and strolling along the surf. (James W. Harrington)

hours patrolling the area surrounding the House of Refuge. A firearm (.45 caliber pistol) was carried by the person(s) on duty from sundown to sunrise. In addition to duty hours, we had to attend daily classes for instruction on various aspects of seamanship.

Off duty hours were spent in various recreation activities among them swimming or playing sports on the beach. Liberty (our time off) was occasionally spent at the movie theater in Stuart or at the Juke Joint located near the wooden bridge in Jensen. A pick-up truck at the House of Refuge served as the base's means of transportation.

After six months at the House of Refuge, I was transferred a short distance up the coast to the Fort Pierce Inlet Station where the officer in charge was Ensign Culpepper, a career Coast Guardsman, who had been promoted from Chief Petty Officer.

With the minor exception of some physical differences in the bases (the tower here was located about one mile away at the Jetty), duties at Fort Pierce remained essentially the same. One change involved the use of dogs to assist the men patrolling the inlet area. In addition to the continuation of our seamanship instruction, we also became familiar with Rescue Boat Operation and, for a short time, cleaned buoys to be used in the Indian River.

When I first went to Fort Pierce Inlet Station, we were the only service group stationed there. Soon after, however, an additional base was installed at the same location by the Navy to train their seamen in the use of amphibious landing craft. As a result of this influx of men and equipment, the inlet area became very crowded. Unfortunately for them, the Navy personnel did not have the quality of facilities that we enjoyed. Whereas their sailors had to stand to eat at boards placed on poles to serve as tables, we ate indoors, family style. Also, we slept on double bunk cots and their accommodations were such that there was very little protection for them from the sand flies.

A few months later, I was transferred from Fort Pierce Inlet Station to Vero Beach Station which was located between Vero and Fort Pierce. The station at Vero Beach had a lookout tower like the others, but the main duty of the guardsmen here was to patrol the beaches on horseback every night from 5 p.m. to 6 a.m.

This photograph of Coast Guardsmen on horseback was taken at Vero Beach. Hutchinson Island also had horseback patrols during World War II. (James W. Harrington)

Upon leaving the station, one rider would go south and another rider would go north. The riders going south would go as far as the Fort Pierce Jetty, then return. Those heading north would go as far as Vero Beach before returning back. Every half hour two more riders would depart, with the last riders leaving the station around midnight.

The timing of this set-up was designed to allow the riders to pass each other in opposite directions at half-hour intervals. However, as the horses we used had been brought out of pasture, they were accustomed to going at whatever pace they wanted, and little could be done to change them.

The patrols were enlivened by the many wild pigs encountered along the beaches as well as the ever-present sand flies. On many nights when there was little or no breeze along the beaches, the sand flies would bite and irritate the patrol dogs to such an extent that it became extremely difficult for their handlers to control the dogs' attempts to escape their tormentors.

But, surprisingly, the greatest discomfort was caused by the cold nights. It seemed to me then that I was colder in Florida on those patrols, than I could ever remember having been in Pennsylvania. On some occasions, I can remember having worn so many clothes that it was difficult to get on the horse.

After having spent about one year at various stations along South Florida's east coast, I was transferred to the Tampa Bay area where I was assigned to security at various docking facilities.

GILBERT'S BAR HOUSE OF REFUGE — HOME OF HISTORY

The Stuart News
January 9, 1964 by Ernest Lyons

The Night Adolf Hitler Hit Us with Torpedo from a Sub
Gulf Stream Tanker Fires Sight of War

Every reporter has at least one story in a lifetime that he never got to print. This is mine.

At 11 o'clock on Saturday night, Feb. 21, 1942, our little town of Stuart, Florida, was shaken as if by the hand of a giant. Houses and business buildings reeled; windows were cracked by the terrific explosion.

I remember being knocked from bed and holding our infant son in the dark, passing him to my wife who made sure that he was safe. "What do you think it was?" she asked. "It was a bomb," I said. "The war has reached us."

Up till then World War II had seemed far away, a distant thing affecting other people. Not us. That was before all the soldiers came to train at Camp Murphy and before the young aviators were practicing night-fighting in their Black Widows at Witham Field. But this was war. There was no mistaking the sound of a war bomb. Maybe it was the St. Lucie river bridge, I thought. Maybe the locks west of town. I pulled on my old clothes. I had been fishing that afternoon, and made my way to The Stuart News office where I found Ed Menninger, the publisher, already at work on the telephone trying to locate the source of the explosion. Soon we were calling all around the county. Yes, they had felt it here and felt it there, but no one knew where it had hit. Then we called Fort Pierce, eighteen miles to the north. They had felt tremors. Okeechobee City, fifty miles to the west, had "shivered." Jupiter, twenty miles to the south, had felt it strongly.

Try as we might, nowhere could we locate the heart of that infernal blast. I went home and to bed and around 1:30 a.m. there came a rap at my door. It was Sheriff

Ernest F. Lyons
(The Stuart News)

Burning ships, torpedoed by German U-boats, were visible along the east coast of Florida in May 1942. (Florida Photographic Archives)

General M. Hancock and Deputy Tom Gardner. "The Germans torpedoed a ship," said the sheriff. "The survivors are coming ashore at Hobe Sound. Come along."

I hurriedly dressed and piled into his car. We stopped off at the Pelican Hotel just long enough to pick up Francis Stan, Washington Star newspaperman, who was here doing a story on sailfishing.

Down at the Worthington Scranton beach house on Jupiter Island the survivors of the SS Republic were coming ashore in the dark, disembarking from the lifeboats — making their way up to the most amazing scene of hospitality I had ever seen in a lifetime of newspaper reporting. There were twenty-four of them — five of them had died in the blast and six eventually made their way to Port Everglades.

From the survivors I soon learned that the ship, a tanker of 5,882 gross tons, owned by the Petroleum Navigation Company, had been struck by two torpedoes, both on the port side.

But it was not the blast that sank the ship that threw us from our beds in Stuart.

"The sub fired three torpedoes," one of the seamen told me. "It was the second and third that got us. The first missed us and plowed into the reef ashore. My God, what a noise it made." That first exploding on the St. Lucie Inlet coral reef, a rocky stratum which extends under the land, had shaken us like a terrier shakes a rat. One of Hitler's bombs in the form of a submarine's torpedo had actually landed on U.S. soil. It was the night that Hitler had tossed a bomb on American soil, even though by accident. I could see the headlines all over the country when I would send out my story on the wires later that morning.

But an even bigger story was unfolding before us as Stan and I interviewed the oil-soaked seamen, busily made notes, getting their names and where they were from.

It was a story of the heart of America. The rich folks on the millionaires' colony on Jupiter Island and the plain folks of the Hobe Sound mainlanders as well were coming to the aid of the rescued men. Vee Chambers of Hobe Sound remembers it. She was there — and helping.

Stricken American seamen needed dry clothing. They needed food and succor. The word went out and into Mrs. Worthington Scranton's beach house with its blacked-out windows facing the sea, came the Islanders bearing gifts. And the mainlanders. There were suits tailored on Bond Street. There were shaggy tweed coats from Scotland. There were two-toned shoes for a trip to Bermuda. Panama hats and lounging jackets. There was plain, simple clothing too, from the mainlanders. Take your pick.

The sailors did. They shucked their dungarees and work clothes. I remember that one hairy-chested fellow was soon wearing a Chinese robe with a dragon embroidered on it in gold thread. A phonograph started blaring a popular song, then switched to a jazz tune. Soon he was dancing with a debutante, rather clumsily, because he was wearing burry Scotch golfing shoes.

There was Scotch. And champagne. And bourbon. A plate of smoked turkey sandwiches appeared. And a ham. And caviar and olives. And cocktail sausages. Soon there was warmth, a sudden bond, good fellowship. I would not have been surprised if the roughneck in the Chinese robe and his new-found girl friend had slipped out for a look at the stars. One Islander even stopped me, where I sat in my smelly old fishing clothes, and said: "You poor boy, let me get you something decent to wear." When I told my wife about this later she said that I had been foolish not to get myself a decent outfit when I had the chance, reporters' salaries being what they were back then.

Stan and I were very happy, as reporters always are when they are sitting on a big story all their own. We could see our by-lines all over the nation later that day depending on who got to the Western Union office first.

The last man ashore was the captain. I already knew his name, Captain Alfred H. Anderson, through pumping the seamen, was prepared to be gracious and quote him in my big story. I can still see his face as I addressed him.

"Captain Anderson," I said, "I represent the Associated Press. Tell me how you felt when that sub..."

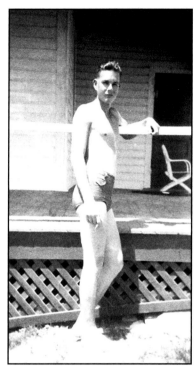

Qurlie Humble of San Antonio, Texas, was dressed in his bathing suit enjoying the surf when Coast Guard Station 207, at Gilbert's Bar, got word that a ship had been torpedoed off Hobe Sound. Everyone hopped into the pickup truck and went to the scene where Qurlie was given a 45 automatic revolver and left to guard the lifeboat the survivors brought to shore. (Qurlie Humble)

"To hell with the Associated Press!" he roared. "Don't you know there's a war on? You can't print one word about this!"

He strode into the room to a coffee table and pounded on it with his fist. "This is no time for a party," he said, contemptuously regarding the Scotch bottles, the sandwiches and the blaring phonograph. All dancing stopped, all eating, all drinking. The place was still. "Have you forgotten those poor devils in the hold? Every man-jack in my crew march outside! The Navy's sending trucks to take us to another ship."

In the dawn Francis and I watched the sobered seamen (well-fed, too, and re-clad for the most part in their dirty and oily work clothes) filing into the grey Navy trucks. I wonder how many of them made it through the war?

There were many another stories that we could not print back in those grim early days of World War II when submarines took a deadly toll of shipping off the Florida coast. Most of our destroyers and sub chasers were overseas, or guarding the vital transport routes. This coast was practically defenseless.

Day after day we watched the rolling black smoke of stricken tankers out on the Gulf Stream sailfishing ground, and there were pillars of fire by night. One sailor — just one of a crew of I don't know how many was pulled from ahead of a wall of blazing oil by a Salerno commercial fisherman. For weeks he lay in our hospital here in Stuart, the sole survivor. He was our boy.

A charred and bloated body was found on the beach. We held a little ceremony for "The Unknown Seaman" out at Fern Hill Cemetery.

The subs were said to be hiding in the dirty water coming out of St. Lucie Inlet from Lake Okeechobee and they could not be seen by aerial spotting. They came up only at night. One loud-mouthed Salerno fisherman bragged: "If I ever see one, I'll ram it with my boat." He returned to port one morning, white and shaken. He had met one on the surface charging its batteries. "Those damned things," he said, "are thr-ee-ee hunn-dred feet long!"

There's the untold story of the Stuart Sailfish Fleet, pressed into service by the Navy and the Coast Guard in one of the most impudent bluffs ever pulled. The charter captains would slip out of port after dark, rev their engines up to highest speeds and cruise up and down offshore. The Coast Guard hoped that the sub skippers would think that the racing boats were armed with depth bombs and submarine detection devices. They didn't even have their fishing rods aboard!

There was the sub that was chased from its lair and destroyed by planes with depth bombs half way between Stuart and Fort Pierce. Witnesses on the shore told of seeing the sub's tail go up in its death dive while they cheered, but we couldn't write it. That wasn't news.

And it wasn't news that marvelous new radar techniques were being taught at the giant Signal Corps installation at Camp Murphy (now Jonathan Dickinson State Park). It wasn't news that Witham Field had been mocked up as an aircraft carrier, dimly lighted where men with fluorescent paddles waved in the new Black Widow night fighters — but what a zing went through our hearts in this little town when the squadrons trained here knocked down eighteen Jap Zeroes in their first night fight. To us, Stuart had turned the tide of battle in the Pacific.

We, our little town, had helped avenge the death of Admiral Kidd, Mrs. Chappelka's brother, at his station on the battleship Arizona in Pearl Harbor on that "day of infamy."

There were many another story that we could not print, because they might give "aid and comfort to the enemy." Also, there was a memorandum from the government, a capricious note, which I tossed idly into my desk (it would be an historic scrap of paper today): "Office of Voluntary Censorship, to all newspapers: never under any circumstances mention the word uranium in any news connection." Never, huh? Who cared? What was uranium? Those guys up at Washington must be nuts.

There were so many stories never printed. But I remember remarking to Francis Stan as we tore up our notes and tossed them out of Sheriff Hancock's car on our way home from Mrs. Scranton's beach house: "There goes the biggest story that I never got to print."

COAST GUARD YEARS

Letter Home Edition Stuart News
October 7, 1943

Oldest "House of Refuge" Has a Happy Crew
Gilbert's Bar Station is oldest in nation, has saved many lives.

Martin County Installation Has Cheated Davy Jones of His Prey Many Times: Chief Lewis is in Charge. The Coast Guard's oldest "House of Refuge" in the United States is located in Martin County.

Gilbert's Bar Life Boat Station, reputed to be 83 years old, and the Coast Guard's oldest "House of Refuge" still in operation today stands high on the rocks in her ancient and stately dignity, touched with the modern art and craft that make her "seaworthy." This old house of refuge for people in distress has seen many ships and sailors in distress and oft times cheated Davy Jones of his prey, even as he stalked his quarry.

The life boat station, too, has seen many periods of transition but still stands sturdily aloof several miles north of St. Lucie Inlet overlooking the Atlantic Ocean to her east, the Indian River to her west.

Since war began, and even before, many improvements have been made. A year-and-a-half ago a new coastal look-out tower was built, a mess hall added and other improvements effected.

SAVES LIVES AND PROPERTY

Constant as the roar and roll of the ocean waves, this old station is steadfast, offering shelter and refuge to those within miles of her "to the rescue" crew.

The men here are a happy crew, know their job and do it. A self bailing surf boat and pulling surf boat are at the command of this crew who stand ready day and night to answer any distress call. Many lives have been saved by being prepared for any and all emergencies.

Crew's sleeping quarters are in the main two-story building. They have plenty of games, sports equipment (five fine rod and reels recently being donated by the people of Stuart), more books and magazines than spare time to read them.

VETERAN IN COMMAND OF STATION

In command of this station is Chief Boatswain Mate Tommie Lewis, a "veteran of 24 years" in the Coast Guard. His varied duties at different stations in which he has been located have given a broad scope of knowledge and experience.

LEARNS MEANING OF SEMPER PARATUS

Soon after enlisting, the value of speed in life-saving was brought home to him when he and his mom rushed out to Charleston Inlet in a motor boat to save the lives of eight men. The old iron-type boat in which the eight men were aboard had capsized and sank immediately, leaving the crew at the mercy of the rough sea without benefit of even a life jacket. Only the speed of "always ready" saved the lives of these men.

Chief Lewis was born in Harkers Island, received his schooling there, married hometown sweetheart, Mary Rose, in 1918 prior to enlisting in the Coast Guard in 1919. Since that time he has served at many different stations. Has been on present assignment two years.

Chief and Mrs. Lewis are mighty proud of their young son, Tommy Livingston, their first, born after 22 years of marriage. Chief Lewis is 44 years young, favorite hobbies, when he can find the time, are fishing and bowling. He also likes baseball.

COAST GUARD YEARS

Led by veteran Tommy Lewis CBM, in command of Gilbert's Bar Life Boat Station, this crew of men are happy Coast Guardsmen all. They work hard, and do hazardous work, gladly and happily, to bring their "V" formation (note picture) to victory.

Back row, up stairway is: Norman N. Jeffry Sea. 1c, Thomas Rex Ingram Sea. 1c, Hugh E. Jordan, Sea. 1c, Nicholas A. Pintado Sea. 1c, Joe Lewis Cox., A. L. Brown SC1c, Tommie Lewein CBM (in command of station).
Front row, left to right is: Charles J. Telesco Sea. 1c, J. W. Gilliam Sea. 2c, William L. Shuppert Sea. 2c, Carl Cohen Sea. 1c, George L. Hamill Sea. 1c, Steve P. Vanno Sea 1c.

(Caption from October 7, 1943, Stuart News*)*
(Florida Photographic Concern photograph courtesy Joyce Gideon Schultz)

An Abandoned Building

Boatswain's Mate 1st Class Bernard Hodapp, Jr., of Stuart, was in charge of nine men at Gilbert's Bar Coast Guard Station as World War II drew to a close. In April 1945, he received orders decommissioning the site that had served the United States government for seven decades. Hodapp lowered the flag and waited for orders.[1] When he left a month later, the former House of Refuge was abandoned to the elements. It was a picnic destination for area residents who either came by boat or traveled south on the trail-like beach road after crossing the Indian River via the rickety wooden bridge at Jensen Beach.

The Segerstroms and friends stand on the porch of the abandoned Coast Guard Station in 1949. From left, Emma Nicholson; Connie Segerstrom and her father, Harry Segerstrom; Robert Whitticar and Edith Segerstrom. (Connie Segerstrom Haire)

The Segerstroms, of Jensen Beach, and friends sit on the beach by the Coast Guard lookout tower in 1949. From left, Connie Segerstrom, Emma Nicholson, Harry and Edith Segerstrom and Robert Whitticar. (Connie Segerstrom Haire)

AN ABANDONED BUILDING

U.S. Coast Guard Station 207, the former House of Refuge, stood abandoned after it was decommissioned in 1945. This was its condition shortly before it was officially acquired by Martin County on January 5, 1955. (Thurlow/Ruhnke Collection)

This photograph, probably taken in 1956, shows the cyclone fence installed by William Cross for the county in 1955. The buildings have been repaired for museum use. When the museum opened, a pioneer kitchen and living room were set up in the "Martin County Building" to the south of the main structure. It also housed the museum archives and library. The main building was used as an art gallery and the former boat house was used to display artwork of public school students. (Thurlow/Ruhnke Collection)

The Creation of a Museum

Charles Val Clear inspired Soroptimist International of Stuart to establish the Martin County Historical Society in order to preserve the House of Refuge for use as an historical museum and art gallery. The Society was created in 1955.[1] Charles Val Clear, who had a background in museum- and art-gallery development, had recently moved to the area and was teaching painting in the basement of Stuart High School. After he had suggested painting somewhere on location, one of his art students, Mabel Witham, introduced him to the deserted House of Refuge and told him of its long and interesting history. Clear immediately saw its possibilities.[2] The county was in the process of purchasing the abandoned government facility. Clear's sister, Zola Swarthout, was a member of the newly-formed Soroptimist club. These elements fell into place to facilitate the creation of the Martin County Historical Society and the development of the House of Refuge Museum.[3]

On January 5, 1955, the U.S. Bureau of Land Management transferred 16.56 acres, including the former House of Refuge, to Martin County.[4] By March 28, 1955, the Soroptimists' project committee had obtained a charter for the Martin County Historical Society. Shortly

Left to right: Charles Val Clear, museum consultant, sits with the first officers of the newly-formed Historical Society, Lillian Armstrong, Secretary, J. Brian Frazier, President, and Lolene Stokes, Vice President. This photograph was taken at the home of Ellen and Mid Nelson on April 4, 1956. (Thurlow/Ruhnke Collection)

THE CREATION OF A MUSEUM

afterward, Clear was appointed art consultant to the House of Refuge Museum by the board of county commissioners.[5]

When the House of Refuge Museum opened to visitors on January 15, 1956, more than 2,000 visitors jammed the narrow dirt road leading to the museum.[6] The museum was formally dedicated in a ceremony at Memorial Park in Stuart on December 9, 1956. Dignitaries spoke and Bernard Hodapp, Jr., who decommissioned the House of Refuge as a Coast Guard station in 1945, raised a flag that was later placed at the museum.[7]

Martin County Commissioners pose at the opening of the House of Refuge Museum on January 15, 1956. Charles Val Clear, the first Director of the Museum, kneels beside a young girl on the porch. Commissioners left to right: Charles Leighton, Seymour Gideon, E. J. Arnold, Earl J. Ricou and Earl G. Knoll. (Thurlow/Ruhnke Collection)

Bernard Hodapp, Jr., who while he was in the Coast Guard lowered the flag over Gilbert's Bar Coast Guard Station in 1945, raises the flag in Memorial Park at the formal dedication of the museum on December 9, 1956. (Thurlow/Ruhnke Collection)

GILBERT'S BAR HOUSE OF REFUGE — HOME OF HISTORY

More than 2,000 people attended the opening of the House of Refuge Museum on January 15, 1956. The cars, parked along the beach road, had to travel across the wooden Jensen Beach Bridge since the "Bridges to the Sea," later named the Evans Crary Sr. Bridge and the Ernest F. Lyons Bridge, had not been constructed. (Thurlow/Ruhnke Collection)

A Refuge for Sea Turtles

Mabel and Ross Witham were very active in the effort to establish Gilbert's Bar House of Refuge Museum. In the fall of 1955, Ross was walking south of the museum and found a baby loggerhead entangled in seaweed. After this chance incident, an intensive plan for the conservation of sea turtles was launched at the House of Refuge Museum.[1]

The Martin County Historical Society requested and received a permit from the Florida State Board of Conservation allowing it to take turtle eggs from the beaches and transfer them to the protected grounds of the museum. The eggs were incubated and the hatchlings were raised in tanks until they were large enough to ensure a better chance of their survival once released.

Facilities for keeping the young were practically non-existent. A small pool was scooped out of the sand and lined with plastic. There was no electricity for a pump, so buckets of water had to be carried from the river. The donation of a gasoline-driven pump and enough plastic pipe to run from the museum grounds to the river inspired the turtle preservationist to set the hatchlings up in a dugout canoe.[2] This illustrates how turtle conservation took precedence over historical conservation.

Nurturing turtle hatchlings was of such priority in the early 1960s that this dugout canoe was used as a turtle tank. (Florida Photographic Archives)

When Stephen Schmidt assumed the directorship of the House of Refuge Museum in November 1958, he placed the Turtle Conservation Project high on the list of the Museum's functions and services. By 1961, two concrete tanks supplied with fresh sea water by an electric pump were installed. Also, the old cistern that formerly supplied the House of Refuge with water was converted into a tank for larger turtles.[3]

Although green turtles were once common in the Indian River, the State Board of Conservation thought the species did not lay eggs in Florida. However, Conservation Agent Roland C. "Boot" Byrd of Stuart found a nest of green turtle eggs in August 1958 on Hutchinson Island and transferred the eggs to the House of Refuge. Soon other green turtles were given a head start at the House of Refuge along with the more common loggerhead turtles. Hawksbill turtles also were hatched and raised successfully.[4]

In 1961, the House of Refuge Museum added stone crab and spiny lobster projects.[5] Sea turtles, however, captured the public's attention and support. Children and the general public became involved. Youngsters were invited to scrub algae from the backs of turtles in the House of Refuge tanks. In 1962, the Stuart-Jensen Elks Lodge pitched in and, with the support of the Historical Society, built an additional turtle tank near the Coast Guard lookout tower.[6]

Initially, turtles were released into the Indian River, but later they were released into the ocean.[7] Eventually, these turtle releases became popular public events.[8] The effort to increase Florida's green turtle population that began with Ross Witham's "headstart" program was seemingly successful. Over 18,000 hatchling green turtles were raised in captivity for six to 12 months prior to their release. Approximately a dozen facilities around the state participated in the program, but the House of Refuge

Ross Witham's life changed one day in 1956 when he was walking on the beach south of the House of Refuge as therapy for a knee injury sustained during WWII. He came across a baby loggerhead turtle entangled in seaweed. The incident inspired a career in marine biology with particular emphasis on sea turtles. This photograph, taken by Ed Gluckler in the early 1960s, shows Ross with a turtle hatched from an egg incubated at the House of Refuge Museum. (Thurlow Collection)

A REFUGE FOR SEA TURTLES

In the early days, HRM (for House of Refuge Museum) and the date of release were carved on the shell. Ross Witham also experimented with different types of paint so released turtles could be identified in a more visible way. An "Adopt a Turtle Plan" encouraged Museum visitors to sponsor a turtle by donating $3 or $4. The patron's number would be painted on a turtle's back and the donor was encouraged to return to the Museum and "watch the turtle grow." (Thurlow/Ruhnke Collection)

served as the main facility. Ross Witham retired in 1987 and the last hatchlings were released the following year. The program had tremendous success in making the public aware of the endangered status of the species.[9]

However, in 1989, the Florida Department of Natural Resources ended the first phase of the headstart program — the collecting, rearing, tagging and releasing of young green turtles. There were some who questioned the effectiveness of the program. Consequently, officials felt it was time for the second phase of the program which would be to await the return of the turtles to the nesting beach.[10]

In 2002, one of the green turtles Ross Witham had tagged returned to nest near Melbourne. When he heard the news, the gentle scientist exclaimed, "I survived long enough to see it happen."[11]

Ross Witham, Martin County's "Turtle Man," died two years later at the age of 87.[12]

Children scrub algae from the backs of sea turtles with tooth brushes in February 1962. (Florida Photographic Archives)

The Ever-changing structures

Repairs and renovations were made to Gilbert's Bar House of Refuge soon after it was constructed and have continued through the years. Salt-laden air is rough on buildings and, as a result, maintenance is never-ending.

Gilbert's Bar House of Refuge was built by Albert Blaisdell of Massachusetts following detailed specifications and was completed on March 10, 1876. It originally had long, open porches on three sides.[1] According to Charles Pierce, who lived at two different houses of refuge as a boy: "All of these houses were built exactly alike, and all of the keepers used the four rooms on the ground floor in the same order as we did. The south room was a bedroom and the next was always used as a living room; the next was a dining room and then the kitchen. North of the kitchen was the cistern, built in the ground and made of brick. Eve troughs led from the house to this cistern, which was the only water supply furnished by the government."[2]

Before long, glass was installed in windows that originally had only brass screen in them.[3] Problems with chimneys required the kitchens to be altered. Jessee Maulden, filling in as Keeper, on November 19, 1879

This photograph of workmen enlarging the upper story of the Mosquito Lagoon House of Refuge shows how Gilbert's Bar House of Refuge was similarly enlarged. Twice as many windows were installed at Gilbert's Bar as were installed at Mosquito Lagoon. (Elwin Coutant)

THE EVER-CHANGING STRUCTURES

This undated photograph of Gilbert's Bar House of Refuge shows a large boat house at the end of the dock in the Indian River, a barn-like structure to the north, and what was probably the original boat house to the south. (Mary Anne Feldhauser)

wrote: "...The dwelling house roof leaks badly — which makes it difficult to keep anything in good condition. The dwelling stands so near the sea that the sea water striking against the house has rusted off the door and window hinges, and the cistern being only walled up eaven [sic] with the top of the ground — and then covered over flat common boards, and the sea water striking the rocks and falling on the cistern run in through the boards making it unfit for youse [sic]."[4]

An August 9, 1883 wreck report involving the schooner *Iola* tells of a near fatal mishap for Capt. Foggard and two sailors. They were in a yawl rafting lumber ashore to be used to repair the House of Refuge when the boat flipped and trapped the two sailors beneath it. David Brown, the Keeper, and his son ran to the rescue and, with the help of Capt. Foggard, succeeded in righting the boat and freeing the men.[5] According to the wreck report in the National Archives, one of the men exclaimed, "If we had been two minutes longer under that boat we would have been dead men."[6]

A photograph taken in 1905 shows two-thirds of the porch on the east side of the house enclosed.

In 1910, Alan Shaw, the son of one of the U.S. Life-Saving District Superintendents whose job it was to inspect houses of refuge, lived at Gilbert's Bar House of Refuge and made repairs. He was in a service branch similar to later-day Seabees.[7] We know he was still at

75

Gilbert's Bar House of Refuge on October 6, 1912 because he wrote his name and the date on the side of the cistern when he either built or repaired it during his stay.[8] Alan Shaw's notation on a photograph in the Historical Society of Martin County archives says, "This is the wall I built."

This is the only known photograph of a lookout tower that stood at the south end of the station. Perhaps it was destroyed in the locally devastating hurricane of Labor Day 1933. (Mary Anne Feldhauser)

The enlargement of the upper story and installation of 24 windows, 12 on each side, probably took place during the time Alan Shaw resided at Gilbert's Bar House of Refuge.

A flimsily built lookout tower appears in 1907 photographs.[9] Different boat houses appear in photographs taken through the years. A large storage-barn-type structure north of Gilbert's Bar House of Refuge appears in early photographs. The boat house that appears in photographs taken of Coast Guard maneuvers during the period 1913 to 1919 probably is not the one that stands today. Perhaps it was destroyed in the Labor Day hurricane of 1933 as was a look-out tower that stood to the south of the Coast Guard Station.[10]

In March 1935, a year and a half after the destructive hurricane, a contract to move the House of Refuge away from the surf, make repairs and build a garage/boathouse was signed.[11] Chief Boatswain Charles Culpepper and his family continued their routines as the house was slowly moved, with block and tackle, 30 feet to the west. Two new elevated cisterns made it possible for indoor plumbing to be installed. A bathroom located in the northeast corner of the building replaced the privy that once stood east of the former boathouse. The boathouse/garage was used to store the Coast Guard truck and a surfboat on a trailer with large rubber tires.[12]

THE EVER-CHANGING STRUCTURES

These photographs, taken on July 11, 1937, show Gilbert's Bar Coast Guard Station after it was moved 30 feet further away from the ocean. Two large cisterns produced running water that flowed by the force of gravity. The new boathouse, built at the north end of the main house, had a concrete ramp and doubled as a garage. (Mae Coventry Axtell)

77

With telephone communication between Coast Guard Stations, resources could be pooled. This was particularly important after the U.S. entered World War II with the bombing of Pearl Harbor on December 7, 1941. By February 1942, freighters were being torpedoed off the coast within sight of Gilbert's Bar Coast Guard Station. Additional men were assigned to the station requiring additional facilities. A new observation tower was constructed as well as a mess hall.[13] A residence was built on the north side of the garage for a couple named Midget. When the Midgets were transferred, the residence was used by others who were assigned to Gilbert's Bar. After the war, the Pitchford brothers moved the building to Pitchford's camp just west of the Jensen Bridge.[14]

Lumber that once enclosed the House of Refuge porch is stacked on the museum grounds during restoration supervised by architect Peter Jefferson in 1975. (Florida Photographic Archives)

After the House of Refuge was purchased by Martin County, it was restored to become a museum. Cypress shingles were put on the exterior. Two concrete turtle tanks were installed on the west side of the former mess hall in 1961.[15] Other tanks were constructed through the years. The former mess hall was used for pioneer displays, then converted for turtle and spiny-lobster research. Later it became the living quarters for a succession of Keepers.

In 1975, major restorations took place, with Peter Jefferson serving as architect and Thomas Sylvester as contractor. The shingles were removed and the north end of the house was extended. The kitchen was reconfigured and a new chimney was built using bricks from the former Shepard estate in Stuart. The house was given a coat of light green paint with dark green trim. Because of numerous repairs, little is left of the original WWII lookout tower other than its design and appearance.

In 1995, engineers discovered the upper story had never been properly anchored to the first floor. With John Foster as architect and John Lindell as contractor, the necessary work was done. The upstairs windows were also restored.

THE EVER-CHANGING STRUCTURES

Major restoration again took place in 1998 with Brad Granfield as architect and Bob McCreary, of Timbergate Building, Inc., as contractor. At this time, the building was stabilized with new pilings and stainless steel anchors. The House of Refuge was given a coat of white paint which quickly peeled and, because of public sentiment, it was painted green with dark trim once again.

By 2001, the wall next to MacArthur Boulevard was in danger of collapsing, so it was removed. A strong retaining wall was built while members of the Southeast Florida Archaeological Society sifted through the soil that was moved.[16]

The hurricanes Frances on September 4 and 5 and Jeanne on September 25 and 26, 2004, toppled the retaining wall on the south side of the House of Refuge, requiring

In 1960, a concrete wall topped with pickets replaced the cyclone fence except along the road on the Indian River side of the building. Around 1965, that section was completed and a cast-iron gate that once served the National Cemetery at Hampton, Virginia, was installed. (Thurlow/Ruhnke Collection)

The two large cisterns built in 1935 were removed when the House of Refuge was restored in 1975. (Florida Photographic Archives)

the museum to be closed. Emergency repairs to MacArthur Boulevard caused a delay in the permitting process. The House of Refuge was still closed when Hurricane Wilma struck on October 21, 2005.

The wall was not rebuilt until 2006. Other improvements were made to the museum complex during the many months the House of Refuge was closed to the public. All of the concrete tanks except the original two were removed, as was the no-longer-used pump house and rusted cannons and anchors. The House of Refuge, Boat House and the former mess hall that had long served as living quarters were repaired and painted. With the removal of concrete tanks and a raised wooden deck, there was enough open space for a large patio of brick pavers. Contrasting pavers show the location of the House of Refuge before it was moved away further from the ocean in 1935. The remains of the original concrete turtle tanks, on the Indian River side of the former mess hall, were preserved to help tell the story of the Sea Turtle Head Start era at the House of Refuge Museum.

The House of Refuge Museum was reopened with special events held on October 16 and 17, 2006. Today, the structures themselves are showcased as artifacts to tell the story of the House of Refuge through its various reincarnations.

Janet Hutchinson, Secretary of State Bruce Smathers, and Anne Young Shepard confer at the Gilbert's Bar House of Refuge 100th Anniversary Celebration, October 10, 1976. (Historical Society of Martin County)

Observation Towers

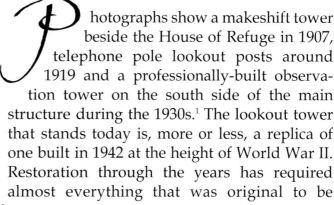

Photographs show a makeshift tower beside the House of Refuge in 1907, telephone pole lookout posts around 1919 and a professionally-built observation tower on the south side of the main structure during the 1930s.[1] The lookout tower that stands today is, more or less, a replica of one built in 1942 at the height of World War II. Restoration through the years has required almost everything that was original to be replaced.[2]

The 1942 tower was similar to others built along the east coast of Florida during World War II and is probably the only one remaining in its original position. Coast Guardsmen assigned to Gilbert's Bar Station took turns climbing the tower and surveying the sky and sea for signs of enemy activity.

Naturally, the tower was not lighted when it was used for surveillance, but on July 3, 1978, a lantern was placed in the lookout tower. The lantern was made from one of the gaslights that once donned the gates of the National Cemetery at Hampton, Virginia. It was placed in the tower as a tribute and memorial to Anne Young Shepard, who was instrumental in the preservation of Gilbert's Bar House of Refuge.[3]

Since October 1984, the Florida Oceanographic Society (FOS) has maintained a Coastal Weather Station in the tower at the House of Refuge. It provides real time weather information 24 hours a day. About 200 boaters, fishermen, and beach goers call in to get a weather report daily. It has continued to operate despite many computer changes. Mark Perry, FOS Executive Director, visits the site almost daily to check sea conditions and surf temperatures.[4]

Although the tower standing next to Gilbert's Bar House of Refuge Museum represents the U.S. Coast Guard era rather than the U.S. Life-Saving Service that occupied the building as a House of Refuge, it has become a popular Martin County icon.

This make-shift tower stood next to Gilbert's Bar House of Refuge in 1907. Edgar Harmer, of Sewall's Point, holds on to the wind gauge with members of the A. L. Andrews family clustered around him. (Agnes Tietig Parlin)

81

Gilbert's Bar House of Refuge with a make-shift tower appears in the distance in this photograph taken from the porch of Gilbert's Bar Yacht Club in February 1907. (Agnes Tietig Parlin)

This photograph taken on July 27, 1950 shows the abandoned former Coast Guard Station. The lookout tower and building to the left, which was used as a mess hall, were built in 1942 at the height of World War II. (Thurlow/Ruhnke Collection)

Louis Bartling

When Martin County applied to purchase the abandoned U.S. Coast Guard Station in 1952, Capt. Louie Bartling was part of the deal.[1] In an official resolution sent to the Department of Interior, the County resolved to take care of William (Louis) Bartling, who had "squatted" on the property, with the help of old-age financial assistance.[2]

It is impossible to verify when Louie Bartling arrived on Hutchinson Island, but Val Clear, Director of the House of Refuge Museum from 1955 to 1957, made a list of Bartling's official documents, certified their authenticity, and transcribed the following statement, "I was shipwrecked at Hutchinson Island in October 1902 and Stanley Kitching picked me up in the shipwreck."[3] The list of documents included a passport stating that Bartling was born in Bremerhaven, Germany, July 4, 1865, and Voter Registration Certificate No. 57 for the Town of Jensen dated November 1931.[4]

Qurlie Humble, who as a Coast Guardsman was stationed at Gilbert's Bar in 1942, reminisced about a nice old gent with an accent who lived near the Station and taught him how to tie knots.[5] Bartling, who trained on the Nautical School Ship *Saratoga* and served on sailing ships, would certainly have been qualified to teach knot-tying.[6]

When the U.S. Coast Guard abandoned Gilbert's Bar House of Refuge, Capt. Louie remained. He was the unofficial caretaker of the former House of Refuge until it became a museum in 1956. Members of the Historical Society felt responsible for his welfare and its lease with the County stipulated that Capt. Louie could remain in his boat-house-shack within sight of the museum for the rest of his life.

Capt. Louie frequently trekked to Jensen Beach to pick up mail and supplies and often flagged people traveling along the beach road and asked for a lift. In reality, he more or less demanded a lift since he stood in the middle of the narrow road.[7] The crusty old former seafarer became a familiar character to the residents of Martin County because sooner or later beachgoers encountered him. Capt. Louie particularly enjoyed visiting the

Sandpiper snack bar at the public beach at Jensen. Carney Forgey, who ran the snack shop in the 1950s, became his special friend. Obviously, Capt. Louie was not expected to read the local newspaper because, on June 7, 1957, the *Stuart News* announced a surprise 91st birthday party for Louie. It would be held at the Sandpiper Inn on July 4 and was co-sponsored by the Sandpiper Inn and the Historical Society. Contributions could be dropped off at the museum or at the snack shop.[8]

When 50 children and 100 adults showered him with gifts and sang "Happy Birthday," the old man's eyes welled with tears. He exclaimed, "This is my first birthday party in my whole life."[9]

On November 19, 1958, Charles Gaye, a toll taker on the new Indian River Bridge, saw an explosion and fire near the House of Refuge Museum. Firemen from Stuart, Jensen Beach and Palm City rushed to the scene, but Capt. Louie's boat-house-shack was engulfed in flames. Fifty firemen painstakingly sifted through the still-hot ashes or searched the shoreline of the river in the vain hope of finding the old man alive. Finally, his remains were found in the kitchen. Investigators determined that his small cooking stove had exploded.[10]

The article about the fire, published on the front page of the *Stuart News* the following day, included a lengthy obituary. Mr. and Mrs. Charles Campbell, a couple who had visited Stuart residents Mr. and Mrs. Steven O'Connor and met Capt. Louie, were in Italy when they read about Capt. Louie's death in the *Rome Daily American*. In January 1959, an item, "Capt. Louie Bartling Got Worldwide Obit," appeared in the *Stuart News*.[11]

One of the earliest loggerhead turtles hatched at the House of Refuge Museum was given the name "Capt. Louie." It grew to an immense size and was on display in the old cistern for years.[12] Capt. Louie Bartling, who lived beside the House of Refuge for decades, was very much a part of its history.

"Old Salt Capt. Lou Bartling, born at Bremerhaven Germany, on July 4, 1865, was the center of attention at a birthday party when 50 children and 100 adults showered him with gifts at 2 p.m. yesterday. The party was held at the Sandpiper at the ocean beach. The Sandpiper furnished cake and refreshments and Captain Bartling received many gifts of clothing, money and furnishing for his houseboat home. Tears came to the old Man's eyes as he said, 'This is my first birthday party in my whole life.' " (Stuart News, July 5, 1957)

Gilbert's Bar House of Refuge Keepers with the Dates of Their Appointments (1876-1910) [*]

Fred Whitehead, December 1, 1876
Jessee Maulden (Acting Keeper, intervals during Whitehead, Stoner and MacMillan's service)
Ezra Stoner, February 8, 1879
Preston McMillan, May 26, 1880
David Brown, December 16, 1881
John Thomas Peacock, February 12, 1885
Samuel F. Bunker, July 11, 1885
David McClardy, June 11, 1888
Hubert W. Bessey, July 12, 1890
Axel H. Johansen, December 28, 1901
William E. Rea, January 2, 1903
John H. Fromberger, May 2, 1907
Axel H. Johansen, April 16, 1910

U.S. Coast Guard Men-in-Charge (1915-1945)

Axel H. Johansen, 1915
Charles Manson, 1918
Charles Culpepper, 1930
Earl Meekins, 1935
Charles Culpepper, 1940
Thomas Lewis, 1941
John Deutch, 1944
Frank Fakes, 1944
Earl Dare, 1944
Bernard Hodapp, Jr., 1945

* Dates are from official records as they are listed in Stephen Harry Kerber's Master's Thesis except that the last date for Axel Johansen is from his oath of office displayed in a showcase in the Old U. S. Custom House, Charleston, SC. Jessee Maulden is on the list because copies of his reports, obtained from the National Archives, are in the archives of the Historical Society of Martin County at the Elliott Museum.

Museum Caretakers — Keepers (Those who served more than a few months) (1955-2008) [*]

Fred Yost, 1955-1956
Stephen G. Bishop, 1957-1964
William and Frances Alloway, 1964-1970
Ralph and Edna Estabrooks, 1970-1972
Richard and Martha Carr, 1972-1975
Christopher J. Nahm, 1975-1976
Ian and Evelyn Butterfield, 1976-1981
David and Dorothy Delk, 1982-1988
William and Jayne Wright, 1988-1993
Barbara Squallante, 1993-1994
Tamara Mayer, 1994-1996
Cynthia Rybovich, 1996-1997
Richard Klug, 1997-2000
Patrick Sheehan, 2000-2001
Katie Rosta, 2002-2003
Linda Geary, 2003-2007
Barbara Dewhirst, 2008-

* Richard Klug's title was Historic Site Manager. From 1997-2003, William Weiss, a Martin County Deputy Sheriff, lived at the House of Refuge. With the hiring of Patrick Sheehan, the title of Keeper was once again given to the Historical Society of Martin County employee in charge of the House of Refuge.

Gilbert's Bar House of Refuge Chronology

("House of Refuge" is used to refer to Gilbert's Bar House of Refuge, Coast Guard Station 207 as well as the House of Refuge Museum)

1871 Sumner Kimball becomes Chief of the Revenue Marine Bureau of the United States Treasury Department including responsibility for U.S. Life-Saving Stations.

1873 Sumner Kimball and Captains John Faunce and J. H. Merryman report to Congress that building and improving life-saving facilities are imperative.

1874 **June 20** — Congress approves recommendations that include building five houses of refuge along the east coast of Florida.

1875 **March 19** — Secretary of the Treasury leases land on Hutchinson Island at St. Lucie Rocks from William H. Hunt for 20 years.

1875 **October 18** — Contract signed for Albert Blaisdell of Massachusetts to construct five houses of refuge.

1876 **March 10** — House of Refuge No. 2, Gilbert's Bar House of Refuge at the St. Lucie Rocks, is completed.

1876 **December 1** — House of Refuge has its first Keeper, Fred Whithead.

1878 Congress separates the Life-Saving Service from the Revenue Marine Bureau and makes it into an autonomous organization. Sumner I. Kimball was appointed General Superintendent of the U.S. Life-Saving Service.

1879 **March 9** — The *Norina* comes ashore ten miles north of House of Refuge. Ten men from the ship are given refuge.

1884 Francis M. Smith receives a contract to build five additional houses of refuge on the east coast of Florida.

1886 **April 19** — The brigantine *J. H. Lane* wrecks five miles south of House of Refuge. Keeper Bunker and two volunteers, H. I. Hawley and Charles Wolf, save the lives of seven men.

1889 **May 23** — Hiram Olds attempts to claim title to House of Refuge land as his homestead.

1890 **December 12** — President Benjamin Harrison reserves Government Lot 2 of Section 5 of Township 38S Range 43E, containing 16.56 acres, for U.S. Life-Saving Service purposes.

1894 **June 12** — Hiram Olds receives a homestead consisting of land to the north and south of House of Refuge but not including the U.S. Life-Saving Service tract.

1904 **October 16** — The 767-ton bark *Georges Valentine* wrecks on the rocks just south of House of Refuge.

1904 **October 17** — The 1,245-ton ship *Cosme Colzado* is stranded three miles north of House of Refuge.

1915 **January 8** — The U.S. Coast Guard is formed from the merger of the U.S. Life-Saving Service and the U.S. Revenue Cutter Service. Gilbert's Bar House of Refuge becomes U.S. Coast Guard Station No. 207.

1916 **November 8** — The *St. Paul,* a 440-ton barkentine, wrecks four miles north of Gilbert's Bar Station. The crew is clothed and taken to Stuart where the owners of the vessel are contacted by telegraph.

1933 **September 4** — Hurricane severely damages House of Refuge

1935 The House of Refuge is moved 30 feet further away from the ocean while the Culpepper family continues to live in the building. Two cisterns and the garage/boathouse on the north side of the building are constructed.

1941 The House of Refuge and all other U.S. Coast Guard facilities come under the direction of the U.S. Navy.

1942 A lookout tower is constructed at the north side of the House of Refuge and a multi-purpose building, originally used as a mess hall, is constructed on the south side.

1945 **April** — Orders to decommission the station are received.

1949 **August 26** — Worst hurricane in area's history demolishes concrete motel units to the south, but the House of Refuge is undamaged.

1952 **June 11** — Martin County Commission resolves to purchase the House of Refuge.

1954 **August 6** — A letter from the acting Director of the Bureau of Land Management stipulates House of Refuge can be purchased by the Board of County Commissioners for ten dollars an acre for a total of $165.60.

1955 **January 5** — United States Government conveys the House of Refuge and 16.56 acres on Hutchinson Island to Martin County.

1955 **March 8** — Charles Val Clear volunteers to assess the possibilities and cost of turning the former Coast Guard buildings into a museum. Martin County borrows money so the needed repairs can be made in a timely manner.

1955 The Martin County Historical Society is chartered through the efforts of Soroptimist International of Stuart.

CHRONOLOGY

The House of Refuge as it looked in 1955. (Bob Cross Collection)

1955 May 10 — The House of Refuge is leased from Martin County by the Martin County Historical Society.

1955 Martin County restores and upgrades the House of Refuge. Shingles are put on the outside of the building and a chain link fence is erected around the facility.

1956 January 15 — More than 2000 people attend the opening of the House of Refuge

1956 Florida Board of Conservation authorizes Ross Witham to collect sea turtle eggs for incubation.

1956 December 9 — The House of Refuge Museum was formally dedicated at the bandshell in Memorial Park in Stuart.

1958 January 8 — Bridges to the Sea on East Ocean Boulevard (to Sewall's Point and Hutchinson Island) are formally dedicated.

1959 First green sea turtle eggs, found by Marine Patrol Officer "Boots" Byrd, were hatched and given a head start at the House of Refuge.

1961 November 18 — The Elliott Museum is dedicated. Martin County exhibits moved from House of Refuge. The House of Refuge becomes a maritime museum.

1964 July — Through the connections of Capt. William R. Laughon, many tons of Navy surplus items were brought to the House of Refuge.

1969 May 29 — House of Refuge is declared an historic memorial in the State of Florida.

1974 May 9 — House of Refuge is listed on the National Register of Historic Places.

1975 House of Refuge is restored under the guidance of architect Peter Jefferson and contractor Tom Sylvester. Porches are reopened and shingles are removed. The house is painted green.

1989 Department of Natural Resources ends the turtle "head start program" at the House of Refuge.

1995	The upper story of the House of Refuge is "tied to the house proper" by contractor John Lindell under the supervision of architect John Foster.	2004	**September 25-26** — The eye of Hurricane Jeanne passes over the House of Refuge. The hurricanes undermine the retaining wall at the south end of the House of Refuge.
1997	**November** — Renovations made possible by a State Historic Preservation Grant and matching funds totaling $289,000 begin. The House of Refuge is stabilized and brought into compliance with the Americans with Disability Act. Brad Granfield is the architect, and Timberlake Construction is the contractor.	2004	**October 16** — Ceremony honoring the men lost on the *Georges Valentine* is held on the beach south of House of Refuge and on a boat over remnants of the ship.
		2005	**October 24** — After making landfall on Florida's west coast, the eye of Hurricane Wilma passes over House of Refuge.
1998	Amateur archaeologists with Southeast Florida Archaeological Society find Ais Indian artifacts beneath and near the House of Refuge.	2006	Turtle tanks and rusted naval-surplus artifacts are removed from House of Refuge site. Brick patio is installed showing the outline of the original position of the House.
1999	**March** — House of Refuge reopens after renovations.	2006	**October 16** — Gala is held celebrating reopening of House of Refuge and dedication of the Georges Valentine Underwater Archaeological Preserve.
2001	A new concrete retaining wall between MacArthur Boulevard and House of Refuge is constructed.		
2004	**September 4-5** — The eye of Hurricane Frances passes over the House of Refuge. MacArthur Boulevard is closed south of Indian River Plantation. Because of this, the House of Refuge is closed.	2008	Publication of *Gilbert's Bar House of Refuge – Home of History*

Endnotes

Overview 1-6

1. Rebecca Harding Davis, "Life-Saving Stations," *Lippincott's Magazine*, XVII (March, 1876) 308-309.

2. Ibid.

3. Sumner I. Kimball, *Organization and Methods of the United Life-Saving Service*, Government Printing Office, Washington, 1890: Treasury Department, *U.S. Life-Saving Service Official Register*, 1886.

4. Sandra Henderson Thurlow, "Lonely Vigils: Houses of Refuge on Florida's East Coast, 1876-1915," *Florida Historical Quarterly*, Volume LXXVI, Number 2, Fall 1997, 154-156; Tax Deed State of Florida to William H. Hunt, November 16, 1876, Dade County Deed Book A, Page 211.

5. Thelma Peters, *Biscayne Country 1870-1926*, Banyan Books, Inc. Miami, Florida, 1981, 16-40.

6. "Gilbert's Bar Named for Rogue, Don Pedro Gilbert, the Pirate," *Stuart News*, January 9, 1964, CC-4; 1934 Map of Florida, Special Collections Department, University of South Florida, shows "Mount Pedro" where Mt. Pisgah stands on Sewall's Point; George Houston 1845 field notes, T38S, R42, Florida Division of Environmental Protection, Bureau of Surveying and Mapping, LABINS Land Boundary Information System.

7. Lovejoy, D.W., *Classic Exposure of the Anastasia Formation in Martin and Palm Beach Counties, Florida*, Southeast Geological Society, West Palm Beach, Florida, 1992, 31.

8. Robert Carr, Archaeological and Historical Conservancy, e-mail to Sandra Thurlow, August 22, 2007.

9. Stephen Harry Kerber, *United States Life-Saving Service and the Florida Houses of Refuge*, Masters Thesis, Florida Atlantic University, 1971, 75.

10. Ibid 197, 124; Charles W. Pierce, unedited manuscript, 162.

11. Thurlow, "Lonely Vigils" 171, "A Story of Gilbert's Bar Station No. 207," *Stuart Messenger*, July 20, 1917.

12. "A Story of Gilbert's Bar Station No. 207."

13. "Jensen Beach is Logical Site for the Coast Guard Station," *Stuart Daily News*, December 2, 1933; "Let Contract on Coast Guard Repairs Jensen," *Stuart Daily News*, March 21, 1935.

14. "Oldest 'House of Refuge,' Has Happy Crew," *Stuart News* (A Letter Home Edition), October 7, 1943.

15. Janet Hutchinson, "House of Refuge," *History of Martin County*, Historical Society of Martin County, 1998, 59.

16. Martin County Commission minutes, November 1, 1944, Book 4, Page 435.

17. "U.S. Speeds Transfer Historic Coast Guard Station to County," *Stuart News*, July 1, 1954; Martin County Commission minutes, December 22, 1954, Book 6, Pages 499, 504.

18. "Soroptimist Leader Lauds Club for Museum Project," *Stuart News*, March 3, 1955; Joe Crankshaw, "House of Refuge Museum Is Two Monuments in One on Oceanside," *Stuart News*, April 14, 1960.

19. U.S. Bureau of Land Management to Martin County, January 5, 1955, Martin County Deed Book 71, Page 552.

20. Martin County Commission minutes, August 11, 1954, Book 6, Page 424.

21. *Florida Historical Quarterly*, Volume XXXV, Number 3, Florida Historical Society, January, 1957, 284.

22. Stephen Schmidt and P. Ross Witham, "In Defense of the Turtle," *Sea Frontiers*, Volume 7, No. 4, November, 1961, 211-212.

23. P. Ross Witham, Resumé.

24. Steve Schmidt, telephone conversation with Sandra Thurlow, June 1994.

[25] "Items Proposed for Shipment to Elliott Museum," February 16, 1960, Martin County Historical Society Archives.

[26] Bunny Abbott, "House of Refuge Museum Gets $25,000 Navy Relics," *Stuart News,* July 9, 1964, 4-A.

[27] Charles Hite, "Martin County House of Refuge Is Getting an Old (1886) Look," *Miami Herald,* January 4, 1976, 2-B.

[28] "A Proposal to Establish the Shipwreck *Georges Valentine* as a State Underwater Archaeological Preserve," Bureau of Archaeological Research, Florida Department of State, February 2005.

St. Lucie Rocks — Hutchinson Island 7-12

[1] *Spanish Land Grants in Florida,* Vol. III, Confirmed Claims D-J, Historical Records Survey Division of Professional Service Projects Work Project Administration, State Library Board, Tallahassee, Florida, March 1941, 300-309.

[2] Treasury Department, U. S. Life-Saving Service Official Registers, Washington D. C., 1880 through 1909, on microfiche at Florida Atlantic University Libraries, list the names of houses-of-refuge keepers and their post office addresses. Copies of the pages of the registers that pertain to houses of refuge are in Historical Society of Martin County archives.

[3] Bureau of Land Management, General Land Office Records, Homestead Certificate No. 10857.

[4] Hutchinson, *History of Martin County,* 57.

[5] "Beach at Jensen Should be Opened Within Few Months," *South Florida Developer,* October 16, 1925.

[6] County Commission Minutes Book 2, Pages 136, 206, 282, 414, 427 and 467.

[7] "Over 2,000 Jam Island Road to See Museum Opening Sunday," *Stuart News,* January 19, 1956; Thomas Thurlow, August 1, 2006, interview concerning the abandonment of the old beach road in Florence M. Barnes vs. Martin County, March 1, 1967.

[8] County Attorney T. C. Houk to Florence M. Barnes, October 24, 1956.

[9] *Stuart News,* January 2, 1958, "This aerial view shows a section of new Highway A1A on Hutchinson Island Constructed by our Firm."

[10] Clifton Perry, interview.

The U.S. Life-Saving Service & Sumner Increase Kimball 13-14

[1] Kerber, *United States Life-Saving Service,* 8.

[2] Davis, "Life-Saving Stations," 306.

[3] Frank Collins Baker, "Sumner Increase Kimball," *Dictionary of American Biography,* 1961, V (part 2) 378.

Keepers of Gilbert's Bar House of Refuge 15-32

[1] Kerber, *United States Life-Saving Service,* 20.

[2] Kimball, *Organization and Methods,* 12.

[3] Kerber, *United States Life-Saving Service,* 20.

[4] Kimball, *Organization and Methods,* 11.

[5] Neil E. Hurley, *Keepers of Florida Lighthouses,* 1820-1939, self-published 1990, 74.

[6] Fred Whitehead to *Anthony's Photographic Bulletin,* July 1877, 318.

[7] Ezra Stoner and the McMillan family were listed both in Brevard County and Dade County, U.S. Census Reports of 1880. The Dade County census stated Stoner was paralyzed.

[8] James A. Henshall, *Camping and Cruising in Florida,* Robert Clarke & Company, Cincinnati, 1884, 75.

[9] Marty Baum, *Ornaments to this Coast,* Letters and Transcriptions Concerning the First Five Houses of Refuge on the Southeast Florida Coast, 1875-1886, unpublished, 2005.

ENDNOTES

[10] Hurley, *Keepers,* 74; Charles W. Pierce, *Pioneer Life in Southeast Florida,* edited by Donald Curl, University of Miami Press, Coral Gables, Florida, 1970, 137. The statement that Maulden would decimate rookeries near Gilbert's Bar House of Refuge is based Pierce's description of what Maulden did on Lake Worth.

[11] Pierce, *Pioneer Life,* 74-75; *Official Registers,* U.S. Life-Saving Service (T2405) on microfiche at Florida Atlantic University Libraries; Fanny E. Brown, "Extracts from Old Letters," *Lake Worth Historian,* published by the ladies of Palm Beach, 1896, 3. Fanny Brown submitted the article from Port Townsend, Washington.

[12] Alan W. Shaw, "House of Refuge," Halifax Historical Society, Daytona Beach, Florida, n.d.

[13] William Emory Rea Obituary, *Stuart Messenger,* September 25, 1924, 2.

[14] Agnes Fromberger to Mrs. Frank Oliver, May 14, 1953, reprinted in (Ft. Lauderdale) *New River News,* April 30, 1974.

[15] "The Gilbert's Bar Mutes," *Stuart Messenger,* August 29, 1918. 1.

[16] Hutchinson, History of Martin County, 59.

Creation of a Museum 68-70

[1] "Soroptimists a Creative Group, News Editor Tells Local Club," *Stuart News,* November 28, 1965.

[2] Mabel Blasko Witham, telephone interview by Sandra Thurlow, July 19, 2006.

[3] "Stuart Soroptimist Club and Val Clear Sparked Historical Society, First Museum," *Stuart News,* November 16, 1961, 7-C.

[4] United States Bureau of Land Management to Martin County, January 5, 1955, Martin County Deed Book 71, Page 552.

[5] Ibid.

[6] "Over 2,000 Jam Island Road To See Museum Opening Sunday," *Stuart News,* January 19, 1956.

[7] "Museum Formally Dedicated Sunday In Impressive Bandshell Ceremonies," *Stuart News,* December 13, 1956, 2-A.

A Refuge for Sea Turtles 71-73

[1] Stephen Schmidt and P. Ross Witham, "In Defense of the Turtle," Sea Frontiers, Volume 7, No. 4, November 1961, 211-212.

[2] Ibid 215-216.

[3] Ibid 216.

[4] Ibid 217-218.

[5] Ibid 219.

[6] "New Elks Club Is Exclusively For Sea Turtles Membership," *Stuart News,* November 8, 1962.

[7] "Rare Trunkback Turtles Hatch Here," *Stuart News,* August 16, 1962, 8-A; Jefferson Siebert, "50 Green Turtles Are Tagged and Released for Return to Beaches," *Stuart News,* April 29, 1973.

[8] "On your marks, get set...," *Jensen Beach Mirror,* May 2, 1984, 12-A

[9] J. Alan Huff, "Florida (USA) Terminates "Headstart" Program, *Marine Turtle Newsletter* 46:1-2, 1989.

[10] Ibid, *Marine Turtle Newsletter,* No. 96, July 1989.

[11] Jim Reeder, "Turtles' return boosts Stuart man's theory," *Palm Beach Post,* August 10, 2002

[12] Joe Crankshaw, "Sea to scatter Witham's ashes," *Stuart News,* March 13, 2004.

Ever-Changing Structures 74-80

[1] *Florida Star,* Titusville, Florida, October 1885. Description of Chester Shoal House of Refuge built to identical specifications.

[2] Charles W. Pierce, *Pioneer Life in Southeast Florida,* 71.

[3] Kerber, "Specifications for Houses of Refuge," United States Life-Saving Service, 116.

[4] Marty Baum, *Ornaments to this Coast.*

5. *Annual Report,* Volume IV, Life-Saving Service, 216.
6. Ibid.
7. Shaw, "Houses of Refuge."
8. "Archeology Reveals Old Cistern at Isle Museum," *Stuart News,* December 4, 1958.
9. Emilie Tietig, list on album of photo negatives.
10. "Jensen Beach is Logical site for the Coast Guard Station," *Stuart Daily News,* December 7, 1933.
11. "Let Contract on Coast Guard Repairs Jensen, Stuart Daily News, March 21, 1935.
12. Sherman Culpepper, interviews by Sandra Thurlow, March 23, 2004 and September 11, 2006.
13. "Oldest 'House of Refuge' Has A Happy Crew."
14. Robert M. Pitchford, interview by Sandra Thurlow, January 28, 1998.
15. Stephen Schmidt and P. Ross Witham, 216.
16. Gloria Fike of Southeast Florida Archaeological Society looking for archeological material, photograph, May 9, 2001.

Observation Towers 81-82

1. Photographs courtesy Agnes Tietig Parlin, Mary Ann Feldhauser and Jennifer Johnson Strauss; "Oldest 'House of Refuge,' Has Happy Crew."
2. Martin County Commission minutes, April 10, 1962, Book 9, Page 553.
3. Bunny Abbott, "House of Refuge Museum Gets $25,000 Navy Relics," *Stuart News,* July 9, 1964, 4-A; Janet Hutchinson, "On the Occasion of Placing the Tower Light at the Gilbert's Bar House of Refuge in Memory of the Late Mrs. William Clark Shepard," July 3, 1978.
4. Mark Perry e-mail to Sandra Thurlow, July 13, 2006.

Louis Bartling 83-85

1. Martin County Commission minutes, June 11, 1952, Book 6, Page 31.
2. Ibid.
3. Charles Val Clear, "Captain Lou Bartling," material copied from his originals. Historical Society of Martin County Archives.
4. Ibid.
5. Quirlie Humble, interview by Sandra Thurlow, December 21, 2005.
6. Clear, Bartling discharge papers from the Pennsylvania Nautical School Ship Saratoga, Philadelphia, Pennsylvania, October 31, 1896.
7. Mabel Blasko Witham, telephone interview by Sandra Thurlow, August 14, 2006.
8. "'Cap'n Lou' Bartling to Have Natal Party," *Stuart News,* June 7, 1956, 1.
9. "Has Birthday Party at 91," *Stuart News,* July 5, 1956, 1.
10. "Bartling Is Fire Victim On Island," *Stuart News,* November 20, 1959, 1.
11. "Capt. Louie Bartling Got Worldwide Obit.," *Stuart News,* 8-A.
12. *The House of Refuge Home of History,* First Federal Savings and Loan Association of Martin County, 1974.

Houses of Refuge Location Map

U.S. Government houses of refuge were unique to the east coast of Florida. Only ten were built and Gilbert's Bar House of Refuge is the only one that survives. This map shows the approximate locations of the houses of refuge as well as the Jupiter Inlet Life-saving Station and their years of construction.

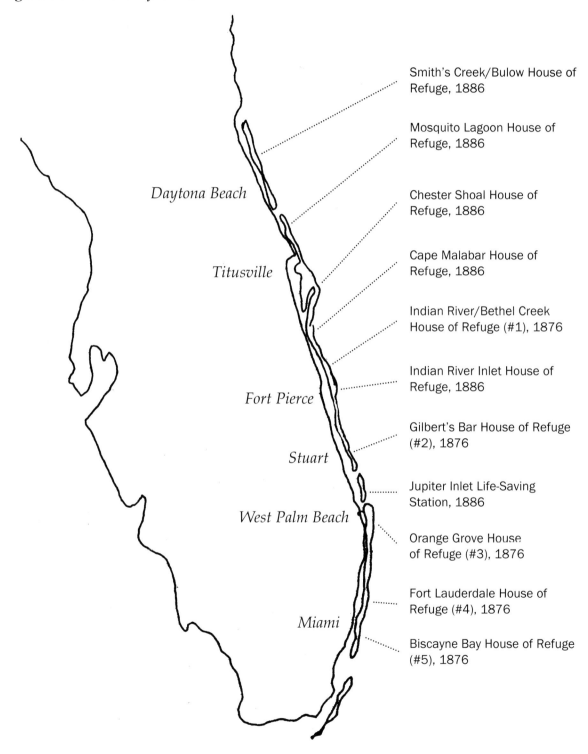

Sandra Henderson Thurlow grew up in Gainesville, Florida, and graduated from the University of Florida. She has lived in Stuart since 1962 when she married Thomas Thurlow, Jr., a young lawyer who had also graduated from the University of Florida. Twenty years ago, when their children, Jacqueline, Jennifer and Todd, were leaving the nest, Sandra turned her energies to collecting and sharing local history. Since Gilbert's Bar House of Refuge is the oldest and most historic building in Martin County, it has always been a favorite subject. This is Sandra's fourth local history book. <u>Sewall's Point — The History of a Peninsular Community on Florida's Treasure Coast</u> was published in 1992, <u>Stuart on the St. Lucie — A Pictorial History</u>, in 2002, and <u>Historic Jensen and Eden on Florida's Indian River</u>, in 2004. Producing <u>Gilbert's Bar House of Refuge — Home of History</u> with her daughter-in-law, Deanna Wintercorn Thurlow, has been a very satisfying and heartwarming experience.

Deanna Wintercorn Thurlow grew up in Stuart and attended Martin County High School where she met her future husband, Todd. She and Todd were married after she graduated from the University of Central Florida and he graduated from the University of Florida. She worked as a society columnist and page designer for the 'Sun-Sentinel' in Fort Lauderdale while Todd attended Nova Southeastern University Law School. Later, when Todd was working toward his master's degree in tax law at UF, she designed the University of Florida 'UF Law' magazine. Deanna has published magazines for a local advertising firm and produced newsletters for the Junior League of Martin County and the Martin County Bar Association. Now the mother of three young daughters, Natalie, Mary and Julia, she has managed to design <u>Gilbert's Bar House of Refuge — Home of History</u> during her limited free time.